PRAISE FOR THE STARTUP VISA:

U.S. IMMIGRATION VISA GUIDE FOR STARTUPS AND FOUNDERS

"There has long been a need for this comprehensive, clear, and insightful resource. Tahmina Watson possesses an unrivaled understanding of the intricacies of immigration law and the potential impact of a startup visa on the American economy. Her book explores the critical need for a new visa category aimed at entrepreneurs and startup founders, while offering creative solutions to the complexities of immigration law.

An important advocacy tool for the public, lawyers, corporations and government agencies, the book distills the complexities of immigration law into an accessible and informative resource.

This groundbreaking work serves as a beacon of hope, inspiration, and guidance for all those who dare to dream and innovate."

— *MICHELE CARNEY, IMMIGRATION LAWYER, CARNEY & MARCHI LAW*

"When companies do not have the requisite information regarding the appropriate visas for their FDI expansion goals, they fall prey to making all sorts of mistakes and eventually stall their company's growth into foreign markets. I will suggest this book to my clients."

— *RITA ADUBRA ASANTE, INTERNATIONAL TRADE EXPERT, HERITAGE TRIAGE GH LTD*

"Immigration issues are a common concern for our portfolio companies. This book gives our founders and us a much-needed (immigration) road map for understanding how to manage and overcome immigration obstacles, so that our startups can get back to focusing on their business at hand."

— *JOANNA LIN BLACK, GENERAL COUNSEL, MADRONA VENTURE GROUP*

"Finally, a practical guide for those seeking a visa to launch a startup company in the US. Tahmina Watson explains the various pathways without the confusing legalese so common elsewhere. Your entrepreneurial journey should begin with this book."

— *WILLIAM BRAH, FOUNDING DIRECTOR, UMASS VENTURE DEVELOPMENT CENTER*

"In over a decade of collaboration with Tahmina Watson, we at Masterplans.com have witnessed the transformative economic contributions immigrants make to our nation. Working with these remarkable individuals, we've seen firsthand their entrepreneurial spirit, diverse skill sets, and innovative prowess, underscoring the urgency for reform in merit-based immigration, country quotas, visa numbers, and H-1B visas."

— BRENT BUTLER, CEO,
MASTERPLANS.COM

"Over the past fifteen years, Tahmina has established herself as one of our country's leading experts on U.S. immigration policy for startup founders. Her book does an excellent job of dissecting an incredibly complex topic and organizing it into simplified chunks that are very easy for the reader to consume."

— PABLO CASILIMAS, CO-FOUNDER AND MANAGING PARTNER AT ONESIXONE VENTURES, SON OF LATINO IMMIGRANTS

"Tahmina Watson is one of the most steadfast and passionate advocates for immigrants I've ever met. Her latest book is a masterclass on active immigration pathways and an insightful analysis of the places where the U.S. visa system falls short."

— WILLIAM T. DEAN, VP IMMIGRATION, MASTERPLANS

"In this newest book, Tahmina provides carefully researched, highly detailed, yet understandable guidance for international founders building businesses in the United States regarding how to move through the visa/immigration cycle as their startup grows. I highly recommend this extraordinary book as a mandatory resource for every foreign-born American entrepreneur, or any native-born entrepreneur likely to need or seek foreign-born talent."

— JOHN DEARIE, PRESIDENT, CENTER FOR AMERICAN ENTREPRENEURSHIP (STARTUPSUSA.ORG)

"At its heart, the book serves as a critical foundation for advocates looking to understand the immigration policy reforms we need in America. It is also a practical tool for those who refuse to be daunted by our present immigration system. This is an invaluable resource for practitioners, policymakers, and dreamers."

— KRISTIE DE PEÑA, SENIOR VICE PRESIDENT, NISKANEN CENTER

"The startup community has needed this book for a long time. There is no one more qualified or committed than Tahmina to deliver it."

— BRAD FELD, FOUNDER, TECHSTARS AND AUTHOR OF VENTURE DEALS

"I truly believe that this book will have an extraordinary impact for decades to come."

— AARON GEORGE, CEO, SUPPLY NOW INC.

"This transformative book, authored by a seasoned entrepreneur and a renowned immigration attorney, is a guiding light for aspiring startup founders in the US. Its comprehensive approach offers practical wisdom and real-world examples while addressing the unique challenges faced by international students who, like me, are pursuing entrepreneurial ambitions in the US."

— ANKIT GONGALE, MBA 2024, WEATHERHEAD SCHOOL OF MANAGEMENT AND PRESIDENT, WEATHERHEAD ENTREPRENEURSHIP CLUB, CASE WESTERN RESERVE UNIVERSITY

"The way Tahmina seamlessly weaves together overarching policies and practical steps is brilliant."

— NICOLE HAY, LAWYER, AUTHOR AND SPOUSE OF IMMIGRANT

"Tahmina's advice and guidance on business visas are invaluable. As a lawyer who works in tech, I know that immigration has been a tough road to navigate over the past few years. You really can't put a price on Tahmina's insights and practical knowledge. This is a must-read."

— JOLEEN WINTHER HUGHES, CEO & FOUNDER, HUGHES MEDIA LAW GROUP

"This book is a call to action for immigrant entrepreneurs, universities, and non-profit organizations to join forces and embrace the benefits of the Global Entrepreneur in Residence program, which empowers international entrepreneurs to work on their startup ideas while contributing to regional economies. Tahmina demonstrates that with the right support and advocacy, talented entrepreneurs can thrive, driving innovation and economic growth in the United States."

— AIJAN ISAKOVA, PROGRAM ADVISOR TO GLOBAL EIR NATIONAL PEER NETWORK

"I have worked with Tahmina for over a decade. We can all celebrate that she is sharing her extensive knowledge on these pages. This book is a must if you are an entrepreneur, founder, or anyone in the startup community."

— GAVIN JOHNSON, CORPORATE ATTORNEY, IMMIX LAW

"Tahmina's book provides readers with clear and concise guidance on the essentials of U.S. visa applications, offering practical strategies to overcome the seemingly insurmountable task of collecting the required documentation. Her commendable efforts deserve recognition for effectively simplifying the visa application process."

— AILSA KAMINSKI, EXECUTIVE PRODUCER - FILM PRODUCTION

"Tahmina's book is a game changer for many startups and founders, not only in the technology industry but in any industry. Your startup will be on a different level because of the access to the US market that the startup visa offers."

— *SRIDHAR KATTA, FOUNDER AND CEO, TRUVS*

"A visa can make or break someone's career or dream. As the leading advocate for the startup visa, Tahmina Watson shares her top-of-the-industry knowledge in this book for entrepreneurs, founders, and investors to take charge of their business goals in America."

— *TANYA KAUSHAL, JOURNALIST*

"Tahmina distills her hard-won experience into this practical guide on immigration law for startups. Her client commitment, knowledge, and passion for service shine through."

— *AJAY KSHATRIYA, EXECUTIVE CHAIRMAN, BARRIER BIOSCIENCES*

"Tahmina Watson draws from her extensive experience to provide a clear and concise understanding of the startup visa options and processes."

— *CHELSEA LINDER, PARTNER, GENER8TOR*

"Tahmina Watson is a wonderful colleague and a passionate and dedicated servant when it comes to immigration visas. *The Startup Visa* will give many the knowledge they need to become part of this country's success story."

— ERNESTINE LYONS, PROGRAM MANAGER, GLOBAL DETROIT

"Tahmina is this perfect combination of policy wonk, startup fanatic, and perpetual optimist all rolled into one. I can't think of a better person to help immigrant founders build their dream startups right here in the U.S."

—PETE MARTIN, HEAD OF CONNECTION, MICHIGAN FOUNDERS FUND

"Tahmina Watson masterfully unveils the transformative power of startup visas, illuminating the path for extraordinary individuals to navigate the complex realm of immigration while building their dreams abroad. As a venture capitalist, I've witnessed firsthand the invaluable contributions made by immigrant entrepreneurs. Bursting with expert insights, practical advice, and compelling success stories, this captivating read is a catalyst for global collaboration and prosperity. Prepare to be inspired, enlightened, and empowered to unleash the true potential of innovation."

— NEAL MODY, VENTURE CAPITALIST

"In this book, Tahmina shares a "road map" on how you can achieve U.S. permanent residency based on your own merits and creativity. You may need "roadside assistance" from an immigration attorney, but you will know where you are when you ask."

— JOEL PAGET, IMMIGRATION ATTORNEY

"Tahmina's experience navigating the system, both personally and as an advocate, makes her the perfect guide to explain and clarify the complexities of U.S. immigration law."

— CLAIRE E. PARSONS, PARTNER AT WOOD + LAMPING LLP, FOUNDER OF THE BRILLIANT LEGAL MIND *BLOG AND AUTHOR OF* HOW TO BE A BADASS LAWYER

"*The Startup Visa* is an informative U.S. visa guide, not only for startups and founders, but also for those exploring paths for long-term residency in the U.S. The book gives a simple breakdown of different visa types, including general preparation guidance for visas, which can be extremely helpful for individuals new to such processes. Tahmina's generous writing clearly reflects her passion for helping immigrants in the many ways that she does."

— MALAVIKA PATEL, BSME, CLIENT

“Watson has provided an eminently practical and informative guide for entrepreneurs, investors, and prospective employees to navigate the current landscape of visa options. In so doing, Watson reemphasizes the case made in her 2015 book that the startup visa is an economic opportunity at the intersection of immigration and entrepreneurship policy. This volume is an essential tool.”

— AVERY PICKARD, POLICYMAKER EDUCATION DIRECTOR, RAIN CATALYSTS (REGIONAL ACCELERATOR & INNOVATION NETWORK)

At Startups Without Borders, we've met thousands of talented immigrant founders who are fiercely disrupting industries against the odds. This game-changing book is not only a fundamental toolkit for them; it's also a cornerstone for the building of a new global economy that values diversity as an asset to solve the world's most pressing problems.

— VALENTINA PRIMO, FOUNDER AND CEO OF STARTUPS WITHOUT BORDERS

“Tahmina brilliantly lays out the nuances in an area of law that is extremely convoluted and complex. She simplifies the law and concepts in a manner that makes it easy for lawyers and non-lawyers to understand. This is a phenomenal resource book and a must-have for every immigration lawyer and entrepreneur.”

— SHAHZAD QADRI, PARTNER, WONG FLEMING

"Tahmina has really brought this home, surfing the waves and swirls of our complex and ever-changing immigration rules, and making them easier for business owners both international and domestic."

— KELVIS QUAYNOR, FOUNDER & CEO, BOH CONCEPTS

"*The Startup Visa* provides an invaluable roadmap for foreign-born founders looking to navigate the complex US visa landscape. Expertly blending practical guidance with inspiring personal narratives, it stands as a testament to Watson's profound understanding of her field. A crucial resource for any international startup journey."

— MOHAMMAD RAHMAN, CHIEF MARKETING OFFICER AND MENTOR, INTERNATIONAL ACCELERATOR

"*The Startup Visa* equips founders across the globe with the knowledge and tools needed to conquer the US immigration landscape, helping them bring their visionary startups to a global stage."

— NIRJHOR RAHMAN, CEO, BANGLADESH ANGELS

"This is a book about winning—it lays out a strategic road map that sets immigrant entrepreneurs and their investors on a course of success for their startups."

— HEATHER REDMAN, CO-FOUNDER AND MANAGING PARTNER, FLYING FISH PARTNERS

"Tahmina Watson is the preeminent voice for international entrepreneurs. No one in this space should do without the knowledge and expertise she shares."

— *JEREMY W. RICHTER, AUTHOR OF* LEVEL UP YOUR LAW PRACTICE

"Tahmina Watson's book is valuable—in many cases, essential—for startup founders and entrepreneurs trying to navigate the U.S. immigration system. The section on new legislation for startup visas is particularly important for the growth of the U.S. economy."

— *MATTHEW SAWYER, FOUNDER, USACCELERATOR AND ADJUNCT PROFESSOR, COLUMBIA UNIVERSITY*

"US immigration law is arcane and hinders our ability to compete. This remarkable work is an essential guide for technology execs and founders to find a path to building their companies and launching products here. This book will help create jobs and keep the U.S. leading in a fiercely competitive global market."

— *MICHAEL SCHUTZLER, CEO, WASHINGTON TECHNOLOGY INDUSTRY ASSOCIATION*

"Tahmina's expertise shines through in every detail she provides to help international founders navigate the intricate U.S. immigration options in an effortless manner."

— *DIVESH SHARMA, FOUNDER & CEO, D GLOBALIST*

"Tahmina's understanding of the ever-changing dynamics of immigration law has been an indispensable resource for our students. She is a fierce advocate for reform, with the practical knowledge to navigate a flawed system. All of this comes together brilliantly in *The Startup Visa.*"

— *ALEX STONEHILL, ASSOCIATE DIRECTOR, UW COMMUNICATION LEADERSHIP*

"As someone deeply involved in assisting EB-1 and O-1 visa applicants, I can confidently say that Tahmina's book is an indispensable resource. Her comprehensive guidance, practical insights, and focus on business success provide entrepreneurs with the necessary tools to navigate the complex U.S. immigration system and strengthen their immigration case. I highly recommend this book to any founder seeking clarity and guidance in their visa journey."

— *DEREK STURMAN, CEO OF PROMO PANDA*

"It has been great working with Tahmina to set up the GEIR program at Global Cleveland. Her expertise has been crucial to configure details about immigration and educate the region on understanding the importance of this program as an important economic development tool. She has been very articulate, knowledgeable, and rational in supporting Global Cleveland build a systematic approach to start this program in 2022."

— *SUPRIYA TAMANG, PROGRAM TRAINING AND DEVELOPMENT MANAGER, GLOBAL CLEVELAND*

"This book proves that Tahmina Watson is a key driver of innovation in the United States. She understands that startup founders are responsible for all net job growth in the U.S. economy, and her work demystifies the process of immigration for all those looking to start and scale their businesses here. She has a gift for explaining complex legal processes in a way that provides startup founders with a clear baseline of their options and a framework for taking action, ultimately empowering people to pursue their dreams."

— TRISTA VAN TINE, CO-FOUNDER AND EXECUTIVE DIRECTOR, MICHIGAN FOUNDERS FUND

"Tahmina Watson cogently tells the story of America's promise as a global leader in innovation, and how U.S. immigration laws can be harnessed to support the entrepreneurs and founders of the future. I have yet to read an explanation as easy to follow as *The Startup Visa* guide. This is a must-read for future international founders seeking to launch in the U.S."

— STEVE TOBOCMAN, EXECUTIVE DIRECTOR, GLOBAL DETROIT AND FORMER STATE REPRESENTATIVE AND HOUSE MAJORITY FLOOR LEADER, MICHIGAN

"This book is an essential read for international founders who are attempting to cut through the US immigration system's never-ending red tape. Tahmina cares deeply about making startup visa information accessible, and her positive outlook on immigration reform is refreshing."

— STACI ZARETSKY, SENIOR EDITOR, ABOVE THE LAW

ALSO BY TAHMINA WATSON

The Startup Visa

Key to Job Growth & Economic Prosperity in America: Second Edition

Watson Immigration Law (2021)

Legal Heroes in the Trump Era:

Be Inspired. Expand Your Impact. Change the World

Watson Immigration Law (2020)

The Startup Visa:

Key to Job Growth & Economic Prosperity in America

Watson Immigration Law (2015)

THE STARTUP VISA

U.S. IMMIGRATION VISA GUIDE FOR STARTUPS AND FOUNDERS

TAHMINA WATSON

WATSON IMMIGRATION LAW

Published by Watson Immigration Law, Seattle, Washington, USA

www.watsonimmigrationlaw.com

This is a work of nonfiction. The content of this book is for informational purposes only and is not intended as a substitute for legal advice. Although the author and publisher have made every effort to ensure that the information in this book was correct at press time, the author and publisher do not assume and hereby disclaim any liability to any party for any loss, damage, or disruption caused by errors or omissions, whether such errors or omissions result from negligence, accident, or any other cause.

Publisher's Cataloging-in-Publication
(Provided by Cassidy Cataloguing Services, Inc.).

Names: Watson, Tahmina, author. | Vosseller, Troy, writer of foreword.

Title: The startup visa : US immigration visa guide for startups and founders / Tahmina Watson ; foreword by Troy Vosseller.

Description: Seattle, Washington : Watson Immigration Law, [2023] | Series: The startup visa. | Includes bibliographical references and index.

Identifiers: ISBN: 978-1-7357585-7-2 (paperback) | 978-1-7357585-8-9 (hardback) | 978-1-7357585-6-5 (ebook) | 978-1-7357585-9-6 (audio)

Subjects: LCSH: Visas--United States. | New business enterprises--Law and legislation--United States. | Start-up costs--United States--Finance. | Emigration and immigration law--United States. | United States--Emigration and immigration. | Admission of nonimmigrants--United States. | Foreign worker certification--United States. | Entrepreneurship--United States. | BISAC: LAW / Emigration & Immigration. | LAW / International. | LAW / Corporate. | LAW / Commercial / International Trade. | BUSINESS & ECONOMICS / Business Law. | BUSINESS & ECONOMICS / Corporate Finance / General. | BUSINESS & ECONOMICS / Corporate Finance / Private Equity. | BUSINESS & ECONOMICS / Corporate Finance / Valuation. | BUSINESS & ECONOMICS / Corporate Finance / Venture Capital. | BUSINESS & ECONOMICS / E-Commerce / Small Business. | BUSINESS & ECONOMICS / Entrepreneurship.

Classification: LCC: KF4835 .W38 2023 | DDC: 342.7308/2--dc23

Caroline Doughty, Managing Editor
Venice Buhain, Editor
Libby Hawken, Editor
Mim Harrison, Editor
Cover design by Raffy Ferras Hoylar
Author's photograph by Michael Doucett

To all my startup clients, both employers and founders, and especially the power women entrepreneurs, I am grateful to have been of service, to have learned from you, advocated for you and been inspired by you.

TABLE OF CONTENTS

Resources

FOREWORD: TROY VOSSELLER

When Joe Kirgues and I cofounded gener8tor in 2012, we had a simple mission: "To be the best partner for a community to invest in its best and brightest." Since then, gener8tor has grown beyond our imagination, and we have changed lives, while helping our communities rethink economic development and innovation. Today, gener8tor operates more than one hundred startup accelerator programs annually across forty-two cities, twenty states, and two countries, working with more than three hundred startups per year. To date, gener8tor has worked with more than one thousand startups that have cumulatively gone on to raise more than $1.5 billion in follow-on capital and employ more than nine thousand people.

We believe that entrepreneurial talent is evenly distributed across race, place, and gender; however, opportunity is not. For the United States to remain the global leader of innovation, we need the best entrepreneurs in the world starting, building, and growing their businesses here.

I am the proud product of immigrant entrepreneurs. As a second-generation American, the topic of immigration is near and dear to me. When my mom immigrated to the United States from Italy with her parents, they pursued the American Dream by starting a tailor shop in Racine, Wisconsin.

At gener8tor, twenty-six percent of our startup founders are first- or second-generation Americans. We regularly encounter immigration challenges and have had to help find solutions to ensure they could stay in the US. In many situations, due to immigration issues, we have lost talented entrepreneurs who were compelled to move to Canada, or back to their home countries.

As a nation, we are subsidizing the education of some of the brightest minds in the world and then effectively deporting them if they want to start a business creating wealth and jobs in the United States. For the software developer, engineer, inventor, scientist, or researcher born outside the United States who graduates from a U.S. university and endeavors to become an entrepreneur, the path is treacherous and oftentimes infeasible.

The U.S. immigration system is archaic and lacks a suitable visa for the modern-day startup founder.

At gener8tor, we needed a policy solution. As we were facing immigration challenges for our startup founders, Tahmina had just published her first book, *The Startup Visa: Key to Job Growth & Economic Prosperity in America.* I was impressed and grateful that someone was addressing this issue. We immediately invited her to Wisconsin from Seattle, and we've been collaborating since.

Tahmina's knowledge, expertise, and passion are evident to anyone who meets her. She draws on her extensive experience and uncanny ability to explain complex immigration law in simple, understandable ways.

Whether you are a startup founder starting your U.S. immigration journey, or a startup company looking for strategies to hire talent, this book is an essential tool for startup employers, founders, and employees.

In the absence of Congress creating a startup visa, Tahmina's visa guidebook for startups and founders will help you start your immigration journey so that you, too, can get closer to your American Dream.

—Troy Vosseller, Co-Founder, gener8tor

IN MEMORIAM

IN LOVING MEMORY OF LORNET TURNBULL

Very few people are lucky enough to have the kind of relationship that I had with award-winning journalist Lornet Turnbull.

Lornet was my editor, friend, and confidant. She edited my first book *The Startup Visa: Key to Job Growth & Economic Prosperity in America* which was published in 2015 and launched at South by Southwest (SXSW) that year. We updated the book and released a second edition in 2021. In between, she helped me write my columns, OpEds, and so much more.

In early 2022, we started writing this very book in your hands, but life circumstances for both of us slowed progress on the project. Lornet was suffering from stage four colon cancer. As she took care of her health, I got busy with my growing responsibilities including as the President of the King County Bar Association in Washington State, in addition to my law firm and case management.

On January 11, 2023, my beloved Lornet passed away. She left behind her husband Steve Haile and other family members. She was 59 years old.

When I met Lornet in 2007, she was a reporter for the Seattle Times. We were working on a humanitarian immigration story. The story didn't complete for many reasons, but in passing, I had mentioned my concern about the potential for a slowdown in the economy, and with it the possibility of laid-off workers, how terminations could affect H-1Bs and possible deportations. About six to eight months later, when the 2008 recession led to mass layoffs, Lornet remembered my prediction and reached out. That was the beginning of our very unique and special relationship. Her trust in me gave and grew my own confidence in myself.

It was soon thereafter that I became a die-hard startup visa advocate. In those early days of our friendship, we worked on a number of issues. One of the stories advocated for H-4 visa holders to have work permits, otherwise known as H-4 EAD. A few months later, the H-4 EAD did become reality.

But most importantly, we worked on the startup visa as stories for the newspaper. When Lornet resigned from The Seattle Times, she agreed to be my editor for my Startup Visa book. And the rest is history.

Lornet empowered people. She empowered them directly by writing about them and helping doors open for those she wrote about. She also empowered people just by being herself. She certainly empowered, encouraged and loved me, making me one of those blessed by her life.

She used to say that I inspired her with my regular dedicated writing. But she inspired, and encouraged me more.

I love Lornet so much. She was the wind beneath my writing wings. But for Lornet, this book would not exist.

WHY THIS BOOK, WHY NOW?

I've been helping startup founders for almost two decades. For the first five to seven years, I didn't see it as a niche. I just loved to work with those who were starting their dream companies, creating new ways to deal with old problems, and in general, doing exciting things. When I started practicing U.S. immigration law in 2006, the immigration laws, particularly those pertaining to H-1B visas, were not as complicated as they are now—though, they seemed complex at the time.

But it was during the 2008-2009 recession that this work took on a deeper meaning to me.

On January 1, 2009, I opened the doors to my own law firm, Watson Immigration Law in downtown Seattle. From day one, my phone was ringing from people who had been laid off from their jobs. Microsoft, Amazon, and Boeing are global names that have a major presence in Seattle. The recession hit everyone. Businesses had to reduce costs and laying people off was one of the main ways to decrease overhead. I can track much of my writing and advocacy to that era. One of my first articles was published in a local South Asian newspaper titled "How to Maintain Status When Laid Off." Many clients I served during that time told me repeatedly that they had the American dream of starting their own companies, but the U.S. immigration system didn't have a path for them.

To each person, I would promise them that I would research an immigration path for their startup dreams. So, while I would work on their cases to ensure they were legally permitted to remain in the U.S., I was also getting deeper and deeper in my research.

It was around that time Paul Graham, founder of Y-Combinator, wrote an essay introducing the concept of a Founder Visa.[1] That idea gained legs when then-Congressman Jared Polis, a co-founder of TechStars, introduced the first startup visa concept in Congress. Polis' fellow TechStars co-founder and renowned venture capitalist Brad Feld, also became an important voice in that discussion.[2]

The research led to eventually writing my first book in 2015, *The Startup Visa: Key to Job Growth & Economic Prosperity in America*. I was fortunate to launch the book at the famous South by Southwest Festival in Austin, Texas.

Between 2015-2016, I was privileged to be part of Hillary Clinton's immigration working group for her presidential campaign. I had high hopes of the startup visa becoming a reality. But those hopes changed with a different administration in office. Between 2017-2020, I was very much trying to protect my clients and community from adverse immigration policies. Those actions are documented in my second book, *Legal Heroes in the Trump Era*. When President Biden won in 2020, my hopes for a startup visa were reignited and I felt compelled to write the second edition of *The Startup Visa* book, which was released in 2021.

But as the year 2021 progressed, hopes dimmed for immigration reform or even just a standalone law for a startup visa. I realized we have to continue to work within the existing system. And that is not easy to navigate.

I realized the book was not enough to tell people what they needed to know. The book is both an advocacy piece, as well as a guide. But it is not a practical guide. So, I launched a podcast by the same name in early 2022. I am so grateful for the support of so many to ensure *The Startup Visa Podcast* became a reality and success.

Therefore, this new book is intended to be a handy guide for investors, founders, and business owners on the visa options they can consider, understand and even prepare themselves without the guidance of a lawyer. It is intended to be a guide to understanding the visa categories that exist in the U.S. when it comes to startups, founders and entrepreneurs, and how to consider the best visa option for each situation.

This book is meant to serve as a guide for those who are looking to bypass the jargon and legal language that is often hard to distill. I hope you will find it useful.

I'll have to add my usual lawyer caveat—this is not legal advice. But as a general handy-dandy book, I know this book will be of service to you.

1

INTRODUCTION

While I started writing this book around December 2021, the many priorities and responsibilities I carried were slowing me down in making progress. However, the worldwide economic downturn kicked off and layoff started slowly in the summer of 2022. Those turned into massive layoffs by October, and continued mercilessly through the start of 2023. Those factors very much motivated me to bring this book to the top of my priority list. People who are on work visas in the U.S. and then get laid off, generally have only 60 days to find a new job and get a new work visa.

In the summer of 2022, I wrote a visa-by-visa guide for people who had lost their jobs, which was published by local business newspaper the Puget Sound Business Journal. That work turned into advocacy and helping people. And it also led to my first ever workshop for self-employed visa options.

This book will be a version of what I teach in the workshops. It is intended to be a starting point for people who are confused about the myriad of choices of visa types in America, only to realize that perhaps nothing is applicable to their situations. I will write about the separate visa categories with tips on how to prepare the evidence.

You can open up the book to any chapter, and hopefully, it will be good information for any stage you are at in your startup journey.

Here's a summary of what you will find in each section:

Immigration Strategies for Startups and Founders (Chapters 2-6):

Strategy is everything, in my opinion. And sometimes, you don't know what you don't know until you are faced with new opportunities or challenges. This section goes over preparation strategies and documentation, the difference between immigrant and non-immigrant visas, how to strategize around your fundraising, and how your visa needs might change as your startup grows. These chapters will help you prepare and be alert as to when your immigration issues will need attention during your crazy busy startup life.

Non-Immigrant Visas, aka Temporary Work Visas (Chapters 7-14):

For some people reading this book, the dream is to enter the U.S. market with your startup idea. Others of you might be students developing your ventures under the guidance of a university. Some of you are already in the U.S. working for big companies and dreaming about starting your own venture, without jeopardizing your current immigration status. Yet others of you are American startup company leaders planning to grow your dream company by drawing from the most skilled and talented workers you can find from around the world. Non-immigrant visas—also known as temporary work visas—can help you get off the ground. But which one do you consider when an alphabet soup of visas are presented to you? In this section, you will learn about the types of non-immigrant visas for people who want to work temporarily in the United States—whether that's one year, or multiple years. Each chapter goes over a different type of working visa, and for what situations those visas work best.

Immigrant Visas, aka "Green Cards" (Chapters 15-22):

You can't renew the temporary visas forever. There are often legal maximum time limits. So, if you plan to stay in the United States indefinitely, you will have to start thinking about a permanent solution. Immigrant visas will lead to legal permanent residence or "green cards" to live in the U.S. The options will vary depending on whether you are a founder or an employee. In this section, you will learn about the types of immigrant visas for people who intend to move to the United States permanently.

Advocacy, Conclusion and Resources (Chapter 23-24):

As you go through your startup immigration journey, you will encounter legal challenges as well as frustrations with the process, procedures and systems. For people who might be dealing with immigration for the first time, this can be distressing and baffling. This section will give you some historical, political and legal context on the pressing immigration issues that need to be reformed at the highest levels of U.S. law in order to best serve the needs of a modern workforce—as well as just for living in a modern world. Additionally, thanks to *Above the Law* for permission to reprint some of my relevant columns on these topics. You may see yourself in those stories and my hope is that the inner advocate within you will awaken to be part of the change we all need to see for a better community, economy, country and world.

IMMIGRATION STRATEGIES FOR STARTUPS AND FOUNDERS

2

PREPARATION GUIDANCE

This book is written with the assumption you will still need a lawyer because any immigration case is far too complicated to teach in one book. It takes years of experience as a lawyer to even write a book like this. But If you are brave enough to try preparing your case on your own, I will not stop you. However, I tell all my clients who pursue this route, to file their case once and devote all their energy to doing it right. It will save time, money and emotional energy later. The ultimate goal is to ensure you can get working on your business so that it can be successful. Here is some general guidance I give to all my clients.

Team work:

When it comes to case preparation, I tell all my clients that we are a team. You know your facts; I know the law. Think of any immigration case as a team sport. Everyone has a part to play and each person must do their best.

Evidence:

Depending on the type of case you will file, the evidence will vary. Sometimes you may spend a lot of time drafting letters about how brilliant you are and asking your mentors and references to edit and sign the letters. Sometimes, you may spend a lot of time finding a document that is difficult to obtain, such as a birth certificate that was not recorded in a timely manner, or that was lost when the government building that housed it burnt down (this happened to my client!). There are many circumstances in which a crucial document can be difficult to obtain. And sometimes, just gathering existing documents can be a tedious task, especially when you are busy trying to run a startup. What you need to keep in mind is that evidence is everything in immigration cases. And your lawyer cannot do their best job, without the necessary evidence. Work with your lawyer to arrange alternative documents if you must. But know that the burden of gathering evidence is always on you and it must be a priority for you during this process.

Declarations:

Gathering reference letters, testimonials, or declarations is a common item in many immigration cases—both family-based and employment-based. For those reading this book, reference letters may be particularly necessary in the O-1, EB-1 and National Interest Waiver cases (NIW). The question that I get asked the most in these cases is how to write the declaration. I often will be asked to provide a sample. Instead, I like to give my clients a simple structure for writing these letters.

There are four components to a winning declaration:

1. Introduction of the author of the declaration.
2. How the author knows the applicant.
3. The author's observation of the applicant's work.
4. Conclusion.

In addition, always include the resume or curriculum vitae of the person writing the declaration. I tell my clients that O-1, EB-1 and NIW are generally a "brag fest." Nothing is too small to brag about. The author should brag about their own accomplishments and also brag about the applicant's accomplishments and add the author's (usually) very lengthy resume. Ultimately, USCIS is looking to see that one of the top people in the industry is verifying that you, the applicant, are also one of the best.

Patience:

For the same reason that you must focus on the evidence, it is also important to be patient. Firstly, patience is necessary for gathering your evidence. Getting frustrated is an easy response for many when lawyers keep asking for the document that you cannot seem to obtain. Talk it over with your lawyer to ensure you discuss the hurdles. There may be alternative solutions to that piece of evidence. But without patience, you will get stressed. My 2023 goal is to ensure everyone around me is less stressed and I urge you to keep that in mind too.

The second reason to be patient is that all the applications I will address below–and most immigration cases in general–are complicated. Once you are able to gather all your evidence, your lawyer will need to assess the documents and ensure they are presented in the manner necessary for that particular type of application. There is an order to the evidence and each item must be listed in an exhibit list, as well as referred to in the cover letter or brief presenting your case. All of it takes time. Work visa petitions or cases can often become two to six inches thick. People don't often realize that the actual act of filing the case, meaning the act of getting the case to USCIS, can take a significant amount of time by itself. The final copies of petitions will get reviewed, copied, scanned, and mailed. So, best to have patience and understanding from the outset. It will make your team relationship go much smoother. I promise.

Focus on funds:

For any case involving business immigration and especially for startups, the concept of "ability to pay" is crucial.[1] The adjudicators of your application will want to know if you have sufficient funds to operate the business and that you will have sufficient funds for your own salary, or your employees' salaries, depending on for whom the application is being filed.

If you do not have angel or venture funding yet, it's important that you fund the business yourself. If your business already generates revenue, that is really important to highlight. A steady stream of revenue will offset the burden of high funding.

Top line evidence:

In every case, I tell my clients to remember three categories of documents, or I call them "headings." No matter what the visa, these will be important to prove. They may get presented in different orders, or have sub-headings but they will always be necessary. The three headings are as follows:

1. Employer: Most work visas will need a sponsoring employer or business entity, even if you are the sole owner of the business. The documentation about the business will fall under this heading. This includes business formation documentation, bank statements (showing that you have adequate funds or revenue), tax returns, office lease, etc. Most lawyers will give you a checklist of what you will need but it's important for you to be able to show that you must have a business that is operational and that you have documentation proving that you have funds to operate the business and conduct payroll.

2. Employment: The adjudicators will want to know what the applicant, whether that's an employee or a founder, will be doing on a day-to-day basis. You can show this by creating a job description. Depending on the visa type, the job description will need to focus on specific issues. For example, if you are filing an

H-1B visa, the focus will be on whether the academic training from a Bachelor's degree is necessary for the tasks you list. Or, if you are filing an L-1A, the focus will be on whether the tasks convey that you are indeed a manager or an executive of the company. I tell all my clients that this is the starting point for any case.

3. Employee: The adjudicators will need to know that the employee, beneficiary, or you (if you are the applicant) will indeed be able to do the job that is being described. For each type of visa, the preparation will be different. For example, for an H-1B visa, the adjudicator will focus on the educational qualifications. For an L-1 visa, among other things, the adjudicator will focus whether the employee has worked abroad for at least 12 months. In the E-2 category, the adjudicator will focus on whether the applicant has the ability and background to operate a business. Each visa will be different, but the elements are similar and the evidence often will be the same.

Application process

I tell all my clients that it is the evidence that wins your case, not the forms. However, the forms are the vehicle for USCIS to accept your application, your fees and place you in a "bucket" or category of visa. On the face of it, the forms may seem simple, but they are indeed deceptively complex. If you check the wrong box, or don't check certain boxes, the application will be rejected. Additionally, USCIS has several processing offices, also known as "service centers." The service center where you file your application will depend on the type of application, and the location of the main office of the employer or startup. This policy can sometimes change and may depend on the employee's work location instead. This is why it's important to read the USCIS website for the filing address every time.

For all non-immigrant visas, or work visas, the application is filed using Form I-129. Each visa type will also require supplemental forms, which will provide USCIS with additional information on your work circumstances.

For all immigrant visas such as EB-1, or National Interest Waivers, the application is filed using Form I-140.

You can expedite your case for an additional fee, generally known as "premium processing." Most lawyers will call this "PP." PP will allow your case to be adjudicated within 15 calendar days. For some immigrant visas, the PP timeline is 45 days.

If you file your case without the PP option, it may take a few months to hear back from USCIS. Processing times are listed on the USCIS website.

The current fees, which are subject to change, are all listed on the USCIS website. If you want to get some background on how political tides can affect fees, please read my article[2] from *Above the Law* on fee changes that I've included in the back of this book.

Requests for further evidence (RFE):

Sometimes the USCIS asks for additional information about your case or yourself. This is called an RFE – a request for further evidence. For example, in an H-1B case for a "specialty occupation," they might ask if the position really requires a Bachelor's degree. Or, if you are changing or extending your visa status, did you maintain status, or did you become ineligible at some point?

If the RFE is requested during your PP period, the 15-day clock will stop while you are responding. Generally, there is a deadline provided for the response. Once you provide the response, the PP period restarts and thereafter you may get an approval, or a denial.

Not every case gets an RFE, and applications can be approved without the USCIS needing additional information.

Action after a decision:

For non-immigrant visas, if you are in the U.S. when you receive an approval of a change or extension of your status, the approval will include an I-94 document that will allow a seamless transition into the status requested. In other words, your new status takes effect without you having to leave the country.

If you are not in the U.S., then you must apply for a visa at the U.S. consulate in your country. You will need to complete a Form DS-160 (non-immigrant visas) or DS-260 (immigrant visas), pay the consulate fees and provide information on the approval notice. Don't forget to bring the approval notice, your passport and other documents to the consulate. Visit the U.S. consulate website for the specific documents necessary. Once you have the visa stamp, you can enter the U.S. in that visa category.

If you receive a denial, your next steps will depend on your visa status and type, and it is imperative you discuss the options and situation with your lawyer. In some cases, you may have to leave the U.S. immediately or risk losing the ability to return, even as a visitor. Much of it will depend on your individual circumstances. In short, talk to your lawyer.

Summary:

In general, it is important for you to be aware of the general preparation strategy so you know the path you will be taking. Sometimes the journey can be long, but it doesn't have to be overwhelming if you have a strategy.

3

BRIEF SUMMARY OF NON-IMMIGRANT AND IMMIGRANT VISAS

There are two main overarching types of visas: temporary and permanent. Generally, the temporary visas are "non-immigrant" visas and permanent ones are referred to as "immigrant visas." Immigrant visas essentially lead to "green cards."

Non-immigrant visas:

A non-immigrant visa is a type of visa issued by a country to individuals who wish to enter that country temporarily for a specific purpose, such as tourism, business, education, or medical treatment. Non-immigrant visas are usually valid for a specific period of time and may have certain restrictions on activities allowed while in the country.

Immigrant visas

An immigrant visa is a type of visa issued by a country to individuals who wish to permanently move to that country and become lawful permanent residents. Immigrant visas are typically issued to individuals who have been sponsored by a family member, an employer, or through other immigration programs, such as asylum or diversity visas.

Immigrant visas allow individuals to live and work in the country on a permanent basis, and eventually to apply for citizenship. Unlike non-immigrant visas, which are usually issued for a specific period of time, immigrant visas are intended for long-term residency and are generally issued for an indefinite period.

U.S. immigrant visa quotas:

It's a good idea to mention at this juncture that the U.S. immigration framework was created in 1990. There are 140,000 employment-based immigrant visas, or green cards, distributed each year. The U.S. sets a limit by country on the distribution of employment-based immigrant visas—that is, no country can represent more than 7% of employment-based immigrant visas issued each year. The number is further divided into "preference" categories—EB-1 to EB-5. Each preference category has its own waiting time based on the country of birth. If you are from a country with a high population, your wait for a green card will be much longer than one who is from a less populated country. For example, citizens of India and China often wait decades to receive their work-based green cards while citizens of European countries don't have to wait at all.

As such, there is currently a very long backlog for people to receive their green cards particularly from India, China, Philippines, and Mexico. This specific issue is far too complicated to go into any depth in this book. However, for purposes of planning for your visa journey as a startup founder, it's important to be aware that your country of birth and application category for a green card will impact your trajectory in the U.S.

Therefore, planning your immigration journey from a timeline perspective is crucial.

General strategy

Usually, one would first try to secure a temporary work visa, such as H-1B, L-1, or others to establish their business in the U.S.

Establishing a business takes time, whether you are scaling a product or providing services to your clients in close proximity, the operations of the business will need close monitoring for growth. Those growth indicators will dictate, at least for some, that there is a business necessity for having the security and stability of living in the U.S. permanently, without the anxiety of renewing temporary visas. Once the business is stable and growing, a green card or permanent visa becomes important.

At the time of writing in early 2023, the green card process takes at least several years, sometimes longer, depending on the type of application that is being pursued and the country of the applicant's birth. In U.S. immigration, country of birth dictates the green card category even if you are a citizen elsewhere. Therefore, the temporary work visa is an important first step because it permits the founder or employee to remain in the U.S. while continuing to work on their business goals.

Each visa has their own time limits in the U.S. For example, the H-1B visa has a 6-year maximum time limit, and the L-1A has a 7-year maximum time limit. As such, an immigrant visa or green card application becomes an important and strategic issue to tackle.

When and how you apply for the immigrant visa also depends on other factors in your business and your life, including the stage of the business growth in revenue and employee numbers, your life goals, any children you have and their ages, and the time remaining on the temporary visas. U.S. immigration laws allow children under 21 to be dependents, but after that, children must have their own independent visas. This is a stressful issue for many visa holders who are also parents.

My general suggestion to my clients is to first put all their focus on starting the company well and setting it up for success. Then, they should put all their energy into securing a temporary work visa. Once the founder is in the U.S., you can assess the green card application strategy based on the factors I mentioned above. I emphasize to all my clients that what is good for business is also good for your immigration case. So, keep growing and strengthening your business. The more successful you are, the better it is for all your applications.

4

FUNDRAISING STAGES IN VISAS

When I started to practice immigration law in 2006 in Seattle, the startup scene was very much alive. Clients—individuals, founders and employers—would come to my office to explore their options for staying in the United States to start a new venture, and not necessarily after fundraising rounds of millions. Rather, many of my clients had come out of Techstars or similar accelerators, to kickstart their new company's development, or they would obtain angel funding for their initial capital.

A few years after I opened my law practice, President Obama's administration gave a lot of weight to entrepreneurship. The Obama administration took active steps to create policies for entrepreneurs in 2012 that was a huge help in having options for clients to file their startup visa cases.

What visa you will apply for will depend on a number of things. Here are some sample questions to consider:

- Is the visa for you, your co-founder or employees?
- If the visa is for you, what is your current immigration status? Do you hold a visa at the moment? Will it allow you to change your status in the U.S?

- If you are in the U.S, how much time do you have between the current visa, the funds raised, and the need to work at the new company?
- Have you raised funds already? How much? Will you raise more in the future?
- Who invested in your company?
- Is your company established abroad? If so, how long did you work there?
- How much of the company do you own?

If you have raised funds or received awards and grants, the visa will depend on the stage of the startup, as well as the amount of funds raised. Here's a quick snapshot of visas that might apply at each round of fundraising.

Pre-seed round:

At this early stage of your company, you may have crowd-sourced from family and friends, or invested some funds yourself. Perhaps you even raised some money from research and development grants, or from city, state or federal grants. You may be an international student, or you may be someone who lives and works abroad on your startup. Or you may be someone in the U.S. on a work visa for a major company, but working on your hobby project on the side with some cool co-founders.

When the company doesn't have much history and no established revenue but a bit of funding (or no funding), here are some visas to consider:

- F-1 Optional Practical Training
- H-1B
- E-2
- L-1
- International Entrepreneur Parole
- Global Entrepreneur in Residence/Global Detroit

Seed-round:

At this stage, you are expected to have some revenue or perhaps a significant round of funding, the product likely has been launched, or getting ready to launch, and you may have credibility in the industry already.

- H-1B
- E-2
- L-1
- O-1
- International Entrepreneur Parole
- Global Entrepreneur in Residence/Global Detroit

Series A and further rounds of funding:

At this stage, the company is established, has a rhythm for operating, has employees and a healthy revenue stream.

- H-1B
- E-2
- L-1
- O-1
- International Entrepreneur Parole
- EB-1
- National Interest Waiver

In the following chapters, I will discuss the various visa categories and the opportunities and requirements of each. But if you know where you are in the startup stage of your company, you could also flip to the corresponding page of that visa in this book.

5

SCALING UP IN VISAS

Once the startup is up and running, and the founders have their visas (if needed), then comes the challenge of recruiting. Though there have been massive layoffs in the tech industry in 2022 and 2023, the issues will likely still remain that there is a huge labor shortage in the American workforce. In fact, it is not just in the U.S.—there is a skilled labor shortage around the world.

Other countries have changed their laws to address this labor shortage. For instance, Canada has created policies to attract skilled immigrants with faster processing and more favorable laws for those with coveted skills. Recently, Australia made some changes to their immigration policies to attract and retain foreign skilled workers. Many countries have created startup visas (read my previous book) and some countries have created Digital Nomad Visas. All of these policies help attract skilled workers.

In the U.S., once you are ready to recruit, you will face challenges for recruiting foreign talent. To all my clients, and especially startup employers, I suggest creating a country-specific recruitment strategy. In fact, I have been making this suggestion for a decade but never really saw anyone truly implement it—that is, until a new airline called Breeze Airways used it to hire pilots during the Covid-19 pandemic. For the record, I do not know anyone at Breeze, I do not know their lawyers and I have not had the privilege of speaking with them. My knowledge is only from media reports.

When most airlines were basically grounded during the pandemic, there was a huge pilot shortage when airlines were finally ready to fly again. Breeze Airways specifically hired pilots on the E-3 visa program, which is specifically for hiring Australians (see chapter 14). The E-3 generally does not reach its cap of 10,500 a year. It was a genius move to have a country-specific recruitment strategy to overcome a shortage in available qualified workers. By thinking strategically and creatively about U.S. immigration laws, this startup was able to scale very quickly and had a market advantage immediately.

That is exactly the strategy all employers, and especially all startups, can use when the time comes for recruiting employees. In chapter 14, I discuss H-1B1 for citizens of Singapore and Chile, TN for citizens of Mexico and Canada, and the E-3 for citizens of Australia. A targeted recruitment strategy may serve you well.

Additionally, the 2022/2023 massive layoffs are an opportunity for startups also. Given the H-1B lottery problems (discussed in Chapter 9), it will continue to be challenging "winning" the H-1B lottery for new employees. In March 2023, USCIS received over 780,000 H-1B registrations for only 85,000 visas. However, there were already many H-1B visa holders that were laid off who were seeking new opportunities. A visa holder must be employed within 60 days of a layoff to remain in valid status in the U.S. Many H-1B visa holders likely would not have considered working for a startup before this situation. Working at Fortune 500 companies is often their dream. But those layoffs brought about a unique opportunity. And when you hire someone who already holds an H-1B visa, you can transfer the H-1B to your company without going through the lottery.

Another strategy to consider, is for multinational companies who may qualify for the L-1 visa for managers or employees with specialized company knowledge. You can transfer employees from a foreign country to the U.S. on the L-1A or L-1B visa. Read chapter 11.

Note that O-1 visas, commonly called the "genius visa," can be applied during any time in the year. Read chapter 13.

And lastly, if you are a startup founder on an E-2 investor visa, it might be worth considering using the E-2 essential employee category to bring key staff from your home country. Read chapter 12.

In summary, when it is time to scale your company, make a mental note to visit this chapter to create a recruitment strategy for your startup.

6

EXITS AND IPOS

The life cycle of a startup will dictate a person's visa options. For many, the holy grail is to have an exciting exit and gallop towards the sunset. That's if you haven't gotten the serial entrepreneur bug!

In chapter 4, I listed the various visas you may consider for each stage of the startup. This is a good time to revisit that chapter, if you need a reminder.

The cycle of a startup company can vary depending on various factors, such as the industry, the type of product or service, and the specific company's goals and circumstances. However, here are some common stages that many startups go through:

1. Idea and concept development: The first stage of a startup is typically when the founder(s) come up with an idea for a new product or service. They may conduct market research, validate the idea, and create a business plan.
2. Seed funding: In this stage, the startup seeks out the initial funding from investors or other sources to help develop the product or service and build a team.

3. Product development: The startup begins to develop the product or service, often with a small team of employees or contractors.
4. Launch: The startup launches its product or service to the market, often with a beta test or soft launch to gather feedback and make improvements.
5. Growth: The startup experiences rapid growth as more customers begin to use its product or service. The team expands, and the company may seek out additional funding to fuel growth.
6. Maturity: The startup reaches a stage of maturity, with a well-established product or service, a large customer base, and a stable team. The focus may shift to improving profitability and expanding into new markets.
7. Exit: The startup may exit through a merger, acquisition, or IPO providing returns for investors and founders.

It's worth noting that not all startups will follow this exact cycle, and some may experience setbacks or pivots along the way.

Additionally, the timeline for each stage can vary greatly depending on the startup's specific circumstances. But no matter how you move from one stage to another, it is imperative you communicate with your immigration lawyer because your visa, and the visas of your employees, will depend on it.

Mergers and acquisitions:

When a startup goes through a merger or acquisition, visas for all the founders and employees will need consideration. The startup company has obligations to their employees for salary and compliance as the sponsor of the visa. Those responsibilities will have to be borne by the acquiring company. And, in some instances, the immigration service, USCIS, will need to be notified. In my opinion, the easiest practice is for the startup to create a spreadsheet of the visa holders (unless you have an HR software program you use) focusing on their visa types and will be an essential component of the negotiations. I find that those leading the company are focused on the "deal" on the table, especially when the discussions become intense. Notifying me, their immigration attorney, often is an afterthought. Sometimes I hear key words during a visa application discussion, when I have to stop and ask questions about possible sale negotiations. But when I do find out, I provide legal guidance during the negotiations.

For example, if the founder or the employees are on an H-1B, L-1 or any other temporary non-immigrant visa, it's important to know whether the new company will be a "successor-in-interest" for temporary visa purposes. The successor-in-interest from an immigration perspective, is an entity that assumes assets and liabilities of the company with which it will merge or acquire. Complying with the immigration rules for each visa holder is part of the liabilities.

If there are green card applications filed, or in process for you as the founder, or for any of the employees, we would have to analyze how to best salvage the hard work and costs that have already gone toward the applications. The stage of the applications–such as whether a Permanent Labor Certification was filed, or a Form I-140 filed–will dictate the next step.

It's important that the company acquiring, or merging with your startup, is aware of immigration liabilities and responsibilities. In an ideal world, those discussions and agreements will be spelled out and included in your sale agreements.

The considerations will be for the following:

- How many visas is the startup sponsoring?
- What type of visas are they?
- What are the considerations and action items of each visa type?
- Are there any green card applications in motion? If so, what stage are they at and what actions must be taken?
- Is the new company a "successor-in-interest" for this particular visa category?
- Do we have to file a new case with USCIS or do we need to make administrative updates to the employee visa file? What are the deadlines for any action necessary?

Initial Public Offering (IPO):

Some startups are able to take the big step of going public. I have not had a chance to join anyone ring the famous Nasdaq bell yet, but if you are reading this book, I hope you will invite me!

An initial public offering, or IPO, is a process by which a private company offers shares of its stock to the general public. This can be done through a variety of methods, such as a direct listing on a stock exchange or a traditional underwritten offering.

During the IPO process, the company's existing federal ID number (such as its Employer Identification Number or EIN) generally would remain the same. This number is assigned by the Internal Revenue Service (IRS) to identify a business entity for tax purposes.

It's possible that the company may need to update its information with the IRS or other regulatory agencies as a result of the IPO, but this would not typically involve the creation of a new federal ID number.

But if a new federal employer ID number is created, then the company's legal counsel needs to review the immigration statuses of the founders and employees, to safeguard the visas and pending green card applications.

In summary, as the startup moves through the cycle of the startup life, it's important you communicate closely with your immigration lawyer.

NON-IMMIGRANT VISAS

7

F-1 AND OPT STUDENT VISAS

One of the most frequently asked questions from international students on the F-1 visa, is whether they can work at their startup companies during their student visa status. The answer is yes—but only at certain stages of their startups and with strategic preparation. A student that fails to pay close attention to their immigration status as they build a startup while in school, can result in delayed visas down the road—or worse.

It is vitally important that you are aware of all the rules of holding a student visa in the U.S. During this time, your best friend must be the Department of Homeland Security website[1] on F-1 visas. In addition, you must stay in close communication with your Designated Student Officer (DSO) at your school. The DSO will update[2] the Student and Exchange Visitor Information System (SEVIS) to record your status. SEVIS tracks and monitors non-immigrant students and exchange visitors, and keeps a record of status. It also provides a way to identify student and exchange visitors who break the rules for possible removal from the U.S.

On-Campus Employment:

F-1 student visa holders are permitted to work. Often these are on-campus jobs, but not always. A DSO can help you make sure that you are abiding by the rules. Employment during this time cannot be more than 20 hours a week during your quarter or semester—Though your hours can increase to full-time during school breaks.

Generally, such work cannot be self-employment and therefore, getting paid through your own startup isn't permissible under the F-1 (at least until you graduate, read below). Having said that, some startup-related work could be considered educational, and in those situations, work authorization may not be necessary. Work closely with your DSO to make sure any work you do is permissible.

Optional Practical Training (OPT):

Optional Practical Training (OPT) is temporary employment, essentially similar to an internship. It is directly related to an F-1 student's major area of study. Eligible students can apply to receive up to a combined 12 months of OPT full-time employment authorization. A student can apply for OPT authorization, both before completing their academic studies (pre-completion) and after completing their academic studies (post-completion). The length of post-completion OPT permitted will depend on how many months of pre-completion OPT the student worked. The combined period cannot be more than 12 months of full-time work.

But if the student did part-time work for pre-completion OPT, that is also a factor in how much time is remaining for post-completion. For instance, if a student worked part-time under OPT for 12 months pre-completion, they could be eligible for 6 months of full-time OPT after they graduate.

Most of my clients who are students working on startups, choose to use their 12-month OPT period after graduation, instead of before.

During the 12-months post-completion OPT period, the law allows unpaid work. Anyone reading this book will know that the early days of any startup is all about lean operations and bootstrapping. Paying yourself a salary in the early days of a startup is not always financially feasible. However, it is a golden opportunity to work on your startup, using your time and immigration status to raise funds from angel investors, venture capital, accelerators and so forth.

I also encourage students to apply for grants and awards, especially since the International Entrepreneur Rule (covered in Chapter 8) has been revived. This period is a good opportunity to ensure you establish a strong business foundation, because that will be important in the next stage of your immigration process.

STEM OPT Extension:

STEM OPT is an extension of the Optional Practical Training (OPT) program for international students in the United States who have completed a degree in science, technology, engineering, or mathematics (STEM) fields. STEM OPT allows eligible students to extend their work authorization for an additional 24 months beyond the initial 12-month OPT period, for a total of 36 months.

To be eligible for STEM OPT, the following requirements must be met:

- Students must have completed a degree in a STEM field from a U.S. accredited institution;
- They must be employed by a company that is enrolled in the E-Verify program;[3]
- The job must be related to their field of study;

- Students must submit a Form I-983, Training Plan for STEM OPT Students, which outlines the student's training objectives and how they will be achieved;
- Employers must provide STEM OPT students with compensation that is comparable to that of U.S. workers who perform similar duties and have similar educational and professional experiences.

STEM OPT provides international students with the opportunity to gain additional work experience and further develop their skills in their field of study. It also allows employers to hire and retain highly skilled workers in STEM fields.

I have spoken with many employers over the years who shy away from hiring students under STEM OPT, because participating in the E-verify program means they would have additional compliance responsibilities. So, for any student reading this who is not a founder, keep in mind that not every employer is enrolled in that program.

However, I would encourage startup employers to consider enrolling in the E-verify program to be able to recruit talented students on STEM OPT and retain them for more than a year.

Founders/entrepreneurs and STEM OPT Extension:

Students on STEM OPT 24-month extension periods can work at their own startup companies—but only as employees. The regulations clearly state that self-employment is not permitted.

The key is to ensure there is an employer-employee relationship. For founders, it is important to have either a board of directors or other shareholders or co-founders, who will have the authority to supervise your work. It is an essential component. For this element, you must work closely with your corporate lawyer to ensure the corporate structure is set up properly and everyone's interests are protected.

This relationship is also important for the training plan outlined in Form I-983. The employer that signs the training plan must be the same entity that employs the student and provides the practical training experience. The employer's representative must sign the form. In this situation, it may be the chair of the board or the co-founder who will supervise the work. The form cannot be signed by the founder seeking to work on the OPT extension for which an application for an Employment Authorization Document will be filed.

Next, ensure the business is enrolled in the E-verify program. Seeking assistance from a human resources expert and an employment lawyer may help so that you can set up fail-proof systems for operations.

Additionally, ensure that the business is related to your major field of study and that you will work a minimum of 20 hours per week.

The startup must be registered and operating legally in the United States, and hold all proper business licenses.

And finally, I mentioned using the initial 12-month OPT to set up the foundation for the business. This is where it is critically important to demonstrate the business is financially able to support the salary of the student seeking STEM OPT.

Curricular Practical Training (CPT):

The law also allows F-1 students to participate in Curricular Practical Training (CPT). CPT requires you to find the training opportunity first and then the DSO must authorize it, annotating the I-20 form. It also is permissible to have more than one CPT authorization at one time.

Though you cannot be self-employed and work on your startup on CPT, it is important you are aware of the CPT rules so that you can be strategic with your OPT. Whether you use CPT or

OPT, it will be a total of 12 months. In other words, CPT time will count against OPT time. Therefore, you may want to strategize how best to utilize these opportunities and which will serve your goals the best.

Planning the next visa option after OPT or STEM OPT:

This is where things get challenging for international founders and why the U.S. needs a specific "startup visa." I make the argument for one in my first book[4], if you haven't read it already. But in the absence of a startup visa, we must explore all the visa options and why this handbook you are reading now is so important for you. As you focus on the success of your startup, the 24-month clock will be running down, and preparing for the next visa option must be part of your business strategy.

In general, the H-1B (covered in chapter 9) is the normal course of action, but it is increasingly difficult to obtain. You can also see if you're eligible for an O-1 visa (covered in chapter 13). Yet another option to keep in mind if you have raised enough funds, is the International Entrepreneur Parole (covered in chapter 8). Additionally, the Global Entrepreneur in Residence Coalition (chapter 10) could provide another good option.

One of the best things about working at your own startup with legal authorization during your OPT, is that you have control over your future, and as the founder you can take the credit when you talk with potential partners and founders. It is an important window to build up your credibility with evidence, that could possibly help toward an O-1 visa (chapter 13).

The OPT period is an important time to build your startup and your own viability as an entrepreneur. Success in the early stages of your startup business will help determine your next visa option.

8

THE INTERNATIONAL ENTREPRENEUR RULE

The International Entrepreneur Rule (IER) is the closest we have to a "startup visa" in the United States. The program arose out of President Barack Obama's executive actions and was finalized in January 2017.

Just like I have done so with the startup visa over the years, I personally dedicated much time and energy to this rule when it was being created—from advocating, submitting comments during the regulatory process, rounding up the community to be voices of advocacy on the issue and much more. You can read my previous book, *The Startup Visa: Key to Job Growth & Economic Prosperity in America, Second Edition,* for more information.

The rule was finalized in January 2017 just as President Obama was to leave office. The next administration all but took away the rule. After much litigation, the rule barely survived. Thankfully, during the Biden era, the rule was revived.[1] And in March 2023, USCIS finally added the program to their policy manual, signaling to entrepreneurs that the program is very much ready for applications.[2]

This program was created with the startup ecosystem and startup life cycle in mind. In my opinion, this option is best if:

- If you are a startup that has raised funds, either through grants and awards, or through angel funding or venture capital (see below for minimum investment limits).
- In 2023, we do not have expedited or premium processing yet. So, these cases can take several months to approve. Therefore, if you have a little time to spare working on a different visa in the U.S., or are on a student visa with some OPT time left, this could be a good option for you.
- If you are a founder that meets the below requirements, but are outside the U.S. who doesn't qualify for the L-1, O-1, or E-2, this could be a great option for you.

I generally tell my clients that as a startup, all the documents that are required for operating your business are the same documents that would be required here. You do not need to generate, create or work towards getting other evidence. In theory, all the evidence should be readily available to you.

What kind of startup will qualify?

The key throughout the rule is "significant public benefit" and "substantial potential for rapid growth and job creation." These two defining phrases shape the rules.

The rules require the startup to show the following:

1. That it was created within the last 5 years of the application filing date OR,
2. It was created within 5 years immediately before the receipt of grants, awards or investment.
3. Must be formed in the U.S. and operating lawfully in the U.S.

4. Must have substantial potential to experience rapid growth and job creation through significant attraction of capital investment or government grants and awards.
5. It excludes small businesses that are intended to generate income for the small business owners and their families.

How can I qualify as an entrepreneur?

USCIS will look for an entrepreneur who is "well positioned to advance" his/her startup. The rules require the entrepreneur to prove two things about themselves:

1. That he/she owns a substantial interest in the startup. This has been defined as at least 10% of the entity at the time of the visa application and the applicant must maintain at least 5% interest throughout the parole period. And,
2. Has a central and active role in the operations of the startup.

Your corporate documentation such as incorporation documents, cap-tables and so forth, will likely have the evidence to show your ownership and position at your company.

What kind of investment in the startup will qualify?

There are two types of investments that will qualify:

1. Capital from qualified U.S. investors with established records of successful investments.
2. Awards and grants from Federal, State or local government.
3. An alternative criteria where one partially meets the above, as long as one provides compelling evidence of potential rapid growth.

To establish you have received the funds, you will need to provide the contracts and agreements of the funds, as well as relevant bank statements.

Who is a Qualified U.S. Investor and what are qualified investments?

1. A qualified U.S. investor can be a venture capitalist, angel investor or startup accelerator. If an individual, must be a U.S. citizen or a green card holder. If it is a fund management organization, it must be located in the U.S. and controlled by U.S. citizens.
2. The investment from a qualified investor must be at least $264,147.
3. The investor must have made similar investments over the last five years of no less than $633,952, and that at least two of the investment entities (startups) have generated at least $528,293 in revenue with average annual growth of 20% OR at least five full-time jobs.
4. The investment must have been received within 18 months of filing the application.
5. The total sum can be a combination of investments made by one or more qualified investors.
6. Investment can be made in the form of "other security convertible into equity commonly used in financing transactions."

It must be noted that all the investment dollar amounts mentioned above will go up with inflation. Depending on when you are reading this book, you will have to visit the USCIS website to ensure you confirm all the dollar amounts in real time.

Additionally, any investment from the founder or their family will not be eligible for the IER.

In general, this is the most important part of rule but also the most challenging part. First, though an angel investor could readily provide evidence of being a U.S. citizen or green card holder, the venture capital firm partners may not be easily inclined to share citizenship status. You should work closely with the investor to ensure they provide as much information as possible.

And second, though investors regularly make investments in multiple companies in their portfolios, ultimately, those companies are separate entities with their own privacy needs and are not obligated to share internal information about their revenue or personnel.

It is important you work closely with your investors to provide as much documentation as you are able, even if it is a declaration from the investors.

What kind of grants or awards will qualify?

1. A grant or an award for economic development from a Federal, State or local government will qualify.
2. It can NOT be a contract for goods or services that looks like an award/grant
3. Minimum sum must be $105,659.

Provide the agreements, copies of checks and bank account statements to prove you received the funds.

What if I don't raise the above amount of money. Can I still qualify?

Yes. The rules provide alternative criteria for applicants who partially meet the above investments. If you have not (yet) raised the required amounts, you can show the following:

1. You have raised a substantial level of investment even if lower than the above amounts.

2. Provide "reliable and compelling" evidence that the startup will provide significant public benefit and has the substantial potential for rapid growth and job creation.

In essence, there is an opportunity to make your case that you have much potential and that you should be given a chance. This is very much a chance to share your story and why your business will make a difference.

How do I apply?

1. A new form has been created for this particular application: Form I-941.
2. Filing fee will be $1,200.
3. An additional biometrics fee of $85 will be required.
4. Must submit biometrics—meaning undergoing fingerprinting and a background check.
5. If in the U.S., you will attend a USCIS field office for biometrics. If outside the U.S., you will attend your local consulate.

Do I need to be earning an income already?

I'm afraid so. The U.S. wants to ensure that you do not become a public charge. As such, the rule proposes that the household income of an applicant is at least four times greater than the federal poverty guideline.[3] That means, if a federal poverty guideline income for a family of three is $24,650, then the entrepreneur will need to show a household income of $98,600 or more.

However, this annual income requirement can be a combination from both the applicant and their spouse. These new provisions will allow the spouse to receive a work authorization.

What happens if my application is denied?

Unfortunately, you cannot appeal such a decision. It is important to remember that this is a discretionary provision and does not confer a right to a "visa." That being said, you can apply again. The USCIS however can reopen a case on its own motion. Should the USCIS wish, the parole can also be revoked or terminated at any time.

What happens when my application is approved?

Once your case is approved, the next steps will depend on whether you are in or outside the U.S. The program is still new so we have not seen too many of these in action, but in theory, this is what is meant to happen:

If you are currently in the U.S. when USCIS approves your application, you must obtain an advance parole document (Form I-512L) and depart the United States before appearing at a U.S. port of entry for a final parole determination by U.S. Customs and Border Protection (CBP).

If you are outside the U.S. (but not Canadian) when USCIS approves the application, you must visit a U.S. embassy or consulate to apply for travel documentation, before appearing at a U.S. port of entry for a final parole decision. Generally, this is called a boarding/travel foil. Reminder that you will be subject to the U.S. Department of State (DOS) rules just like any other visa background check.

If you are a Canadian traveling directly from Canada to a U.S. port of entry, you may present an approved Application for Entrepreneur Parole (Form I-941) at the U.S. port of entry without first obtaining travel documentation from DOS.

I reiterate that this program is new and your patience navigating these steps will be important. But if this is the best option for you, persevere through it.

Can my co-founders file too?

Yes. However, only up to three founders can apply from the same startup. This is in line with the Invest Visa provisions from the comprehensive immigration reform bill 2013[4] and later bills.

How long will I get to stay in the U.S. on this parole?

You will initially be permitted to be in the U.S. for 2.5 years. You can apply to renew the parole and will receive 2.5 more years. Hopefully by then, your business will be established enough to move on to a different immigrant or non-immigrant visa category—but you may have to leave the U.S. to get the new parole.

What about my family?

Your spouse and children will be allowed to get parole too and live with you in the U.S. They will have to use the traditional application form I-131 and also go through biometrics and background checks. Children under 14 don't have to pay the $85 biometrics fee though. The current administration has been mindful of family unity.

What kind of work authorization will I get?

Thankfully, the administration has thought this out well. Work authorization will depend on approval. That means you will get permission to work, without having to apply for the traditional work authorization that can sometimes take up to 6 months to receive, which could hinder your startup. For human resources and Form I-9 purposes, the parole will be stamped to show work authorization and together with your passport, you will be able to prove that you have permission to work. The Form I-9 is an official form a business must keep on file to demonstrate they have verified that their workers are eligible to work in the United States.

Your spouse will have to apply for work authorization in the traditional way though using form I-765 and pay the appropriate fees. There will be no work authorization for children.

Do I have compliance issues to note?

Yes. Any major events or developments affecting the performance of the startup—referred to as "material changes"—must be reported immediately. Material change could be a criminal charge, conviction, plea or any other criminal case or government administrative proceeding against the entrepreneur or the startup. Also, if at any time your ownership falls below 5%, your parole can be terminated or revoked.

How do I apply to renew parole?

If you want to renew your parole, you must to do the following:

1. File another Form I-941 within 90 days of expiration of current parole. Timing is important or else your parole will be terminated.
2. To qualify, your business must still be a startup and you must still be an entrepreneur as described above. You will have to prove the following.
3. You have received additional qualified investment during the parole period making the total investment $528,293. And;
4. Generated annual revenue of $528,293 with at least 20% average growth during the initial parole period. OR;
5. Created at least 5 full-time jobs for at least 35 hours a week, for workers that are U.S. citizens or green card holders.

What if I don't meet all the requirements for re-parole?

Fear not. The government has thought of this too. If you cannot meet the requirements fully, then you will have to show "reliable and compelling" evidence that you have accomplished a substantial amount of the re-parole requirements as mentioned above.

Can I work while my parole is pending?

Yes. Consistent with other non-immigrant visa categories, you will receive 240 days work permission while your re-parole application is pending.

Are there circumstances under which I could lose my parole?

Yes. Parole can be terminated at any time if USCIS decides that your startup no longer serves a significant public benefit This could be at any time, even without notice. There also will be automatic termination at the end of the parole period or if your equity drops below 5%. If you receive a notice of intent to terminate, you will get 30 days to rebut any allegations.

If there is a violation that results in termination of parole of your spouse or child, you can still remain in the U.S. The violator will not be able to remain.

Summary:

The IER is a wonderful opportunity for the true startup. While it is a relatively new program, it is worth keeping this option at the top of your list.

9

H-1B VISA & CAP-EXEMPT H-1B VISAS

Quick tips:

- This visa is best for you if you have at least a Bachelor's degree.
- Your company has received, or is about to receive, substantial funding.
- You are already in the U.S. on an H-1B visa and are ready for your own startup.

Who should consider this:

- If you are on a student visa, F-1 and subsequent optional practical training (OPT).
- If you have been selected in the lottery already, file your application.
- If you are on an L-1B visa (specialized knowledge). L-1B visas are for five years and cannot be extended. Often it is better to switch to an H-1B and strategize on Permanent Labor Certifications (PERM) and green card applications.

- If you are on an International Entrepreneur Parole, it would be good to move on to an H-1B for more flexibility, especially if you do not yet qualify for an O-1 visa.

What is the H-1B visa?

The H-1B visa is a non-immigrant visa that allows U.S. employers to temporarily hire foreign workers in specialty occupations. The visa program is designed to help companies fill positions with highly skilled workers.

The H-1B visa is valid for up to three years and can be extended for an additional three years. The visa holder may also be eligible to apply for permanent residency (commonly called a green card) while on the H-1B visa. And if a green card application has been filed, the founder or employee can extend the H-1B beyond six years when certain milestones have been met.

The H-1B visa program is highly competitive and subject to an annual cap on the number of visas that can be issued each year. The law allows for a total of 85,000 visas a year in total, 20,000 of which are earmarked for those who have a Master's degree from an accredited U.S. university.

The window to apply will open mid-March of any given year. The lottery will be conducted between March 30th - April 1st. And if selected, applications must be filed by June 30th.

In recent years, it has been challenging to *win* the lottery because the number of applications keeps rising. In 2022 (fiscal year 2023),[1] USCIS received almost 500,000 applications. At the time of writing this book in 2023 (fiscal year 2024), USCIS received over 780,000 applications. With such low odds of winning this lottery, H-1Bs may not be the first choice for many. So, all the visa options in this book must be considered carefully.

Bachelor's degree requirement

To qualify for the H-1B visa, the foreign worker must have a bachelor's degree or higher in a specialized field such as engineering, mathematics, science, or computer programming. The H-1B visa is used in almost every industry for professionals, including teachers, doctors, technology professionals, architects, scientists, and so many more.

For those who are new graduates applying for an H-1B for the first time, they may not have their degree certificates when the first H-1B application is filed in March. That is okay. However, they must have finished all the work to complete their degrees, with evidence of their transcripts and certificates when the application is field.

But what if you or your worker do not have a degree? Sometimes there are talented founders who did not complete university because their ideas took off in the middle of their studies. There are many examples in the world of successful people without college degrees. Richard Branson, famous British entrepreneur and investor, never received a degree. Bill Gates dropped out of Harvard to found Microsoft. Luckily, if you've had practical experience in the profession in which you are trying to work in the U.S., there are ways around this requirement.

Sometimes you may have a degree in one field, but realize that the job you studied for is not for you. So, you may have started working in a completely different field and become an expert in something that you never formally studied in school. Or, perhaps you finished high school and fell into a vocation that you have been practicing for many years and now have an opportunity to be hired on an H-1B visa. A good example is someone who may have been a bookkeeper for fifteen years, but now has the opportunity to be an accounts manager or budget officer on an H-1B which may require a bachelor's degree in finance. If the worker does not have the requisite degree, equivalent experience may be counted towards a degree. Three years of work experience can be the equivalent of one year of academic training, according to the U.S. government.[2]

The salary:

Employers must also demonstrate that they will pay the H-1B worker the prevailing wage for the job. This is done in two ways. First, by filing what I describe as a "promise to pay wages" through the Department of Labor's Form ETA 9035, or Labor Conditions Application (LCA). The DOL has a database of job codes for almost every job. DOL also has a database of what profession should receive what salary based on geographic location and level of experience required. The LCA requires information about the job title, job code, location and wage level for experience. The LCA must be filed through their online FLAG system which can take up to 10 days. DOL certifies the application which then is part of the H-1B application paperwork.

The second part of the evidence is financial documentation from the business to prove the business is financially able to pay the salary. This evidence can be funds that the startup founders capitalize from their own money, or it can be funds raised from investors, or it can be a demonstration of revenue already generated for the business. Sometimes, it can be a combination. The facts of your case will determine the documentation required.

But what if you don't have sufficient funds in the business for a full-time salary? Startup founders will often tell me that they can afford the prevailing wage for the worker they want to sponsor, but only if it is part-time. I'm here to tell you that it is absolutely possible to have a part-time H-1B and make your funds last longer. For example, if the DOL states a full-time doctor must receive $100,000 per year, the DOL will also state an hourly rate for that position—let's say it is $48 per hour. That doctor could work part-time at $48 per hour. The key is to ensure the visa worker is earning sufficient income to not appear to be a "public charge," that is, someone who may be likely to rely on public benefits, such as housing or food.

Two H-1Bs at the same time (Concurrent H-1Bs)?

I will often be asked if someone can work for two companies at the same time on an H-1B. Most often these are founders who launch their hobby into a commercial entity. With the above part-time explanation, it is possible to hold two H-1B visas at the same time.

Let's take the doctor's example again. Dr. Piggy, who holds an H-1B visa, works at hospital New Sesame Street full-time, or 40 hours a week. Dr. Piggy has the opportunity to help a stealth health-tech company at Pink Kermit Lab on some amazing revolutionary innovation in medicine and wants to work for Pink Kermit Lab as well. But Pink Kermit Lab is not ready to sponsor full-time and Dr. Piggy is not ready to leave her full-time job. In this situation, Pink Kermit Lab can file a part-time H-1B for Dr. Piggy and she can work with both companies. It is important to mention that a person cannot hold different types of visas at once, such as a part-time H and a part-time O.

Concurrent H-1Bs are also possible when you have a cap-exempt H-1B. See below for more details.

H-1B Basics for founders:

The most common question I receive from founder clients is whether someone can have an H-1B visa sponsored by their own company. The answer is yes. The key issues, of what can sometimes be referred to as "self-employed" H-1B visa, are the following.

Employment agreement with your company:

If you are the founder/co-founder, you must have an employment agreement with your company. In essence, just like you would have a contract with any other employer, you must do so with your own company.

The founder must be supervised. Someone else must be able to "hire, fire, and supervise you." This could be your co-founders, other shareholders or board members. I've done this in many different ways for my clients. The best solution depends on the facts of the case. Quite often I work closely with the corporate attorney on the structure of the company on this particular issue. For example, if the founder is the majority shareholder, is there anything that can be done to move around the ownership structure? Would non-voting shares be an option? If you add a board, do you need to allocate some share to the board advisors? Corporate attorneys are our best friends in these situations to ensure everyone's rights are protected, especially the founder's, and that we can find the best solution for immigration purposes.

Employee for tax purposes:

You should not be a "contractor" for payroll purposes. You must be an employee and be taxed as an employee. In other words, you will need a pay stub that shows all the usual tax deductions that a U.S. employee receives.

Job title and description:

I cannot tell you how much I agonize over the job title for founders. There is a real need for the founder to often have the title of Chief Executive Officer (CEO). Founders will often tell me that to continue to raise funds, they need to appear to be in charge of the company or they will lose trust or opportunities from investors. But when it comes to H-1B visas, it is very important to ensure that your job title and description mirror your educational background very closely. For example, an architect cannot perform the duties of a doctor because they do not have the academic training for it. Therefore, your academic training and work experience, will be the foundation to describe the duties you will be performing. While I have successfully obtained H-1B visas for founders with the title of CEO, sometimes it can be beneficial to have the title of CEO/expertise.

Cap-Exempt H-1B visa:

When Congress passed the Immigration and Nationality Act of 1990 and created the H-1B program with a lottery, a category was created for H-1Bs that would not be part of the lottery. These H-1Bs are exempt from the annual cap and thus are referred to as "cap-exempt" H-1Bs which can be filed by cap-exempt employers. There are 4 types of cap-exempt employers:

1. Higher education institutions;
2. Non-profit research companies;
3. Government research organizations; and
4. Non-profit entities with higher education institution affiliations.

When a cap-exempt employer files an H-1B visa, it can be anytime in the year. Cap-exempt H-1Bs are often used by professionals in the medical or teaching profession. My clients have included teachers, therapists, counselors, researchers and many more.

The H-1B application for cap-exempt H-1Bs are prepared almost exactly the same way as discussed above. The additional evidence is to prove the sponsoring employer is cap-exempt with evidence of non-profit status and higher educational institution contracts.

More importantly for the purposes of this book, cap-exempt H-1Bs can be used for founders and entrepreneurs. Read the next chapter on Global Entrepreneur in Residence Coalition and Global Detroit.

Concurrent H-1Bs for cap-exempt and cap-subject H-1Bs:

I mentioned above that you can have two H-1Bs at the same time. In addition to the benefit of having a cap-exempt H-1B any time in the year, the other crucial benefit of the cap-exempt H-1B is that you can hold a second concurrent H-1B for a company that would otherwise be part of the lottery. For example, if Dr. Piggy's employer hospital New Sesame Street is a cap-exempt employer, Dr. Piggy can work at Pink Kermit Lab also on a concurrent H-1B, even though Pink Kermit Lab is a for-profit company that would otherwise need to apply for the H-1B in the lottery.

Global Entrepreneur in Residence Coalition has helped many entrepreneurs in this manner.

Filing timelines

Timelines are the most important consideration of what type of visa to file, when to file and how long it will take for the application to be approved. And if the person is outside the country, you must also consider how long it will take to obtain the visa stamp from the consulate abroad.

The H-1B application can be filed in the United States as a "change of status." For example, if you are a student on an F-1 visa, the timeline considerations are generally centered around the end of your educational course, or any optional practical training time (OPT). If your OPT expires after April but before October of that year, you could be entitled to "cap-gap," meaning you can continue to work until the H-1B visa has been adjudicated, or until September 31st if approved. This applies to all H-1B visa applicants regardless of being a founder or not.

I will often ask my clients to create their own immigration timelines while they are students, so they do not miss milestones and significant dates.

What are the best strategies for preparing H-1B visas?

Preparing an H-1B visa application can be a complex process, but here are some strategies that can help:

1. Start early: The H-1B visa application process can take several months, so it's important to start early and allow plenty of time for preparation.
2. Gather all necessary documentation: Make sure you have all the required documentation, such as educational degrees, work experience letters, and proof of specialty occupation. Ensure that all documents are accurate and up to date. See chapter 2 earlier for preparation guidance.
3. Consult with an experienced immigration attorney: An experienced immigration attorney can help guide you through the H-1B visa application process, help ensure all required documents are in order, and help address any issues that may arise during the process.
4. Determine the prevailing wage: Employers must offer the H-1B worker the prevailing wage for the position. Make sure to research and determine what that amount is.
5. File the application during the designated filing period: The H-1B visa program is subject to an annual cap, and applications can only be submitted during a designated filing period each year. Make sure to file the application within the specified time frame.
6. Provide clear and concise job descriptions: Make sure to provide a clear and concise job description that outlines the specific duties and requirements of the position.
7. Anticipate potential issues: Be aware of potential issues that may arise during the application process, such as Requests for Evidence (RFEs), and prepare accordingly.

By following these strategies, you can increase your chances of preparing a successful H-1B visa application, whether you are sponsoring a visa for yourself as the founder, or if you are a startup founder sponsoring talented workers who can further the mission of your company.

10

GLOBAL ENTREPRENEUR IN RESIDENCE PROGRAM

The origin story:

When all efforts for immigration reform failed in 2013, I started to work on my first startup visa book to continue my mission of changing these laws for the better. At the same time, my dear friend Craig Montuori, with whom I was working closely on immigration reform issues, embarked on a journey to help entrepreneurs find a practical pathway to entrepreneurship in the U.S. His vision and hard work resulted in the creation of the Grants (GEIR).

Montuori co-founded Global EIR as a non-profit organization along with strategist Chris Nicholson, venture capitalists Brad Feld and Jeff Bussgang, in 2014. Board members include Shiza Shahid of the Malala Foundation, Heather Redman of Flying Fish Ventures, and many other prominent leaders in the startup ecosystem.[1] I have been privileged to serve as the Chair of the Legal Advisory board since its inception.

The program framework:

In essence, Global EIR connects universities with entrepreneurs and their employees who can conduct research or teach classes.

Nonprofit organizations with university affiliations (such as Global EIR's regional branches) or universities themselves, can apply for H-1B visas outside the annual cap. The program helps universities and nonprofits to allow international students or entrepreneurs to work part-time for the schools, while their ventures are in the idea or the early stages. And once their startup is viable, they will apply for a concurrent H-1B as a founder for their own startup. I will elaborate further below.

Latest reports show that the Global EIR program's entrepreneurs have raised over $1.5 billion in venture funding and created over 2,750 jobs. The footprint is astounding for such a young program. Below are the three models of Global EIR:

1. Employment by the university:

In this model, the Global EIR partner university will employ the international student at the end of their F-1 Optional Practical Training time period. As you learned in chapter 7, the OPT period can be for 12 months or 36 months in total, depending on whether one holds a STEM degree or not.

The international student will be a member of the staff at the university. Depending on the discipline of their own education, the student-turned-staff member will have an appropriate position with the university. For example, many of these positions have included in their job description, that the GEIR entrepreneur teach entrepreneurship to other students. Some of these GEIR entrepreneurs have worked on practical projects at the university, undertook co-teaching, advised student entrepreneurs, operated entrepreneurship labs, advised professors interested in spinning out, and much more. These programs have had a multiplier effect in making the universities more attractive to students to join and brought the universities closer to the startup ecosystem. The impact has been visible and exciting.

Once this cap-exempt H-1B has been secured, the entrepreneur can then apply for a concurrent H-1B with their own company.

2. Employment at the university:

In this model, the international student will be petitioned by their own company by virtue of the locating the company or an office, or doing 51% of their on campus of the university. By working at the location of the university, and proving that the entrepreneur's work will further the mission and goal of the university, the requirements for the H-1B will be met. Examples could include working at the labs of universities for scientific research and experiments for which the university location is imperative. This model works well for life-science and biotech startups.

In this situation, the entrepreneur is already working for their own company and a concurrent H-1B with the university is not necessary.

3. Employment at a nonprofit organization with a higher-education institution affiliation:

Though a newer model in the GEIR framework, the more common cap-exempt H-1B program in general involves nonprofit organizations that have formal relationships with higher education institutions. This is generally more common because the application of the cap-exempt H-1B visa is widely used in school districts, medical clinics, and many other nonprofit settings where hiring and training the next generation of professionals is a regular part of the business. In the Global EIR program, the eligible nonprofit, such as a regional economic development organization, employs the entrepreneur to perform duties of an H-1B-appropriate position. The position will depend on the organization, its mission and the entrepreneur's academic background.

Concurrent H-1B for entrepreneurs:

Once the cap-exempt H-1B is secured, a concurrent H-1B by the entrepreneur's company can be filed. Read chapter 9 about H-1B visas.

In each of these situations, the entrepreneur is given the opportunity to work on their company with valid work permission that would not be otherwise available.

University and organizations involved:

The first university to turn the model into reality was the University of Massachusetts — Boston's Venture Development Center (VDC). Initially led by William Brah, and now by Bala Sundaram, Vice Provost for Research and Strategic Initiatives, the VDC has supported 81 founders who have raised $1.5 billion in venture capital and created some 2,500 jobs. Sundaram told me that the program is so successful that it cannot keep up with the applications from entrepreneurs and investors who want to participate.

The following universities have participated in the program since its launch in 2014.

1. University of Alaska Anchorage (with participation from University of Alaska Fairbanks and Alaska Pacific University)
2. San Jose State University
3. University of Colorado, Boulder
4. Illinois Institute of Technology
5. Northwestern University
6. Columbia College
7. DePaul University
8. Loyola University
9. Babson College
10. University of Massachusetts Boston

11. University of Massachusetts Lowell
12. University of Michigan
13. Wayne State University
14. Lawrence Technological University
15. Michigan Technology University
16. College for Creative Studies
17. Cleveland State University (in partnership with Global Cleveland running the program)
18. Case Western Reserve University (CWRU)

Example of founders:

There are some amazing founders that have gone through the Global EIR program. Below are a few examples:

Nigel Sharp, CEO and co-founder of Aquagga, lives in Tacoma, Washington now. Nigel, a British citizen and founder of Lionsharp, was building interactive multimedia solutions while in the United Kingdom but had funders in the U.S. The funding required that he move to the U.S. to work on the company. There wasn't a suitable visa for him until Global EIR partnered with University of Colorado, Boulder. The partnership allowed Nigel to secure a cap-exempt H-1B. He eventually obtained his green card before he started his current venture.[2]

Aaron George, founder of Supply Now in Cleveland, Ohio, started to fill a void when the Covid-19 pandemic struck. Due to the lockdowns, restaurants were suddenly on the brink of shutting down. Many, in fact, did close down. Aaron realized that the public who were under lockdown still wanted food for takeout. But the restaurants that wanted to serve their customers couldn't get the supplies and food they needed because of the disruptive effects of the pandemic on the workforce and manufacturers suddenly prioritizing much needed medical equipment. Aaron created a tech solution helping restaurant owners find the supplies they needed. And thus was born Supply Now.

Aaron was still on his student visa and optional practical training period (OPT). As discussed in Chapter 7, the STEM OPT does not allow self-employment. But Aaron had co-founders and a board of directors. He was able to work throughout his OPT lawfully with the requisite structures in place. But when it came to moving away from the student visa, the H-1B lottery didn't seem promising. With almost 500,000 H-1B applications filed in 2022, chances were slim of being selected. In fact, 2023's H-1B lottery confirms the concern was real. In 2023, USCIS received over 780,000 applications. There was less than 10% chance of anyone's case being selected. And that leaves entrepreneurs like Aaron in a big black hole with no visa to move on to.

Global EIR helped Aaron secure a cap-exempt H-1B with Global Cleveland, a nonprofit that is lifting the regional economy of Cleveland. Once Aaron secured his visa with Global Cleveland, he was able to apply for his concurrent H-1B. Aaron and his business are now able to confidently grow, create jobs and contribute to the economy.

In October 2022, I had the privilege of attending a Global EIR convening organized by Global Detroit. About ten of the founders who have gone through the program attended. They were all so brilliant, talented and each had a compelling story. All of the founders categorically said that without Global EIR, they could not have started their own companies. In fact, they recall that they likely would not have been able to stay in the U.S. Indeed, those who have been lucky enough to find out about this program, have confirmed the invaluable role it plays in the lives of international entrepreneurs, the dreams and the ripple effect on their surroundings.

Global Detroit and the current state of Global EIR:

In 2017, Global EIR started a close collaboration with Global Detroit in Michigan. Global Detroit is a nonprofit that has proven itself invaluable in helping the local economy of Detroit rebuild after the terrible financial hardship the city went through during the 2008 recession. Through astute leadership and perseverance, Global Detroit helped the local economy and businesses revive. And one of its goals was to harness the energy and talent of international students. Led by Executive Director Steve Tobocman, a former Michigan state representative and a leading visionary in the U.S., Global Detroit's collaboration with Global EIR has been significant. As a result of the strength and alignment of its mission, vision and collaboration, Global Detroit has emerged as a leader in the entire program of Global EIR.

Steve Tobocman's skillful leadership is evident from the incredible team he has been able to put together. Aijan Isakova, the VDC program director, is now working with Global Detroit as the Global EIR National Peer Network Coordinator as the program expands. Ernestine Lyons, a former Director of Legislative Policy for the City of Detroit, is now the Global Entrepreneur in Residence Program Manager. The other team members are equally impressive.

Global Detroit[3] has connected local entrepreneurs with part-time employment at the University of Michigan, Wayne State University, and the College for Creative Studies. In just two and a half years, it has supported eight founders from seven companies who have raised over $15 million and created over 50 jobs.

The benefits of the Global EIR program:

Without the Global EIR program, none of the founders or entrepreneurs would have been able to stay in the U.S. But once they were able to secure their H-1Bs, as their businesses grew, their credibility did as well. It allowed the founder to move on to an O-

1 or EB-1 or National Interest Waiver to move on from the H-1B and/or receive a green card. In essence, it provides a pathway that would otherwise not exist. In the absence of a startup visa, Craig Montuori and his colleagues have achieved a practical way to ensure talented immigrant entrepreneurs can remain in the U.S and grow our economy.

As a side note, I want to take a moment to acknowledge the Global Cleveland team—Nancy Janis, Joe Cimperman and Supriya Tamang. Their hard work in creating a platform and recognizing the value of immigrant opportunities to rebuild local economies is commendable and exemplary.[4]

All immigrant entrepreneurs, universities, investors, and nonprofits with a focus on regional economic growth, should know about this program and find ways to collaborate.

11

L-1 INTRACOMPANY TRANSFEREE

Quick tips

- The L-1A visa is best for you if you have an established company abroad.
- As the founder, or the first employee to be sent to the U.S., you are an executive or manager of the business.
- You have been working at the company for at least one year.

What is the L-1 visa?

The L-1 visa is a non-immigrant visa that allows international companies to transfer certain employees from a foreign branch to a U.S. branch, for a temporary period of time. This visa is designed for employees with specialized knowledge or managerial/executive experience.

There are two types of L-1 visas: L-1A and L-1B. L-1A visa is for managers or executives who are being transferred to a U.S. branch to work in a managerial or executive capacity. L-1B visa is for employees with specialized knowledge in the company's products, processes or services.

To be eligible for an L-1 visa, the employee must have worked for the foreign company for at least one year within the past three years and must be coming to the U.S. to work for the same company, or a subsidiary, parent, branch or affiliate of the foreign company. How established a company is in the U.S. can determine the initial length of the visa. An L-1 visa for someone working in a new company's U.S. office, is issued only for one year initially.

For a more established company that has been around in the U.S. for longer than a year, an L-1A visa can be granted for up to three years and can be extended up to a maximum of seven years and an L-1B visa can be granted for up to five years. The L-1 visa also has a benefit for family members who plan to accompany the visa holder to the U.S. Spouses and unmarried children under 21 years of age can get L-2 visas to enter the country. I'll describe the L-2 visa in more depth later in this chapter.

With maximums of seven years for an L-1A visa and five years for an L-1B visa, it is important to strategize on your long term immigration goal shortly after the initial approval. Firstly, time flies fast when you are busy. Once you arrive in the U.S., you may be so engaged in your new role that you will not have much time to think about immigration until the expiration date approaches. A good strategy will combine your business goals with your immigration goals—whether that means thinking ahead about permanent residency options, or it could mean making plans to leave the United States for at least a year after the L-1 expires. Secondly, a strategy, even an informal one, will influence the choices that you make in your job and life, and the opportunities you pursue.

Preparation guidance

I tell my clients that there are five broad categories of documentation that we will need to gather. Most of the documents are likely to be easily available. However, you have to make sure you devote enough time to gathering them. Founders and executives can often delegate the tasks to a trusted employee.

Qualifying relationship: The starting point for any L-1 visa application is whether the foreign and U.S. entities are "related" or have a "qualifying relationship." Therefore, business ownership documents are among the most critical to collect. Qualifying relationships can include that the foreign entity owns the U.S. entity as a parent company, or vice versa. Or, it could be that the ownership of the two entities are the same or similar resulting in an "affiliate" relationship. Or, that there is a branch office abroad. The law does allow "joint ventures" but those are trickier to prove. Each of these types of relationships can be shown through common corporate documents, so you'll need to gather those as evidence.

Foreign office documents: We must prove that the office abroad is active and operating. We do that with documentation that the office abroad needs to operate the business. That would be a business license, tax returns, office lease, etc. The type of business it is will dictate what additional type of documentation we will need.

U.S. office documentation: To prove that the U.S. office is operational, we will need to gather all the documents that are required to operate the business. This includes state and city business licenses, tax returns, or any other documents required. For example, restaurants may need additional food-related licenses. If you're coming to establish a new U.S. branch of an international company, an office lease is essential. It is important to have leases that demonstrate square footage of the space you have. A mailing address will not suffice. The U.S. government assumes the employees will work at the office. Though Covid-19 greatly expanded the prevalence of working from home offices and normalized remote work teams, for immigration purposes, it is important to ensure you prepare your case with the assumption that employees will work from an office and therefore, you should have an office lease.

In addition, if it is a new office , there will not be much financial history. Therefore, a strong business plan becomes an important component of the application. A business plan will describe in detail the type of services or goods the business will provide, the financial projections and more. This will allow the immigration officer to see the vision of the founders.

Job description in foreign country: The next documents to focus on are job descriptions. To adjudicate the case, the officers will want to know from the job description that the L-1 employee has been indeed acting like a manager, executive or person with special knowledge of the business in their company role. Most of the time, for founders, we will use the L-1A manager or executive category. In this situation, it is expected that a manager or executive makes high level decisions and supervises other employees who carry out other duties, such as admin or programming. It is also important to have job descriptions for both the executive and other staff members that they manage. The job description for other staff members will corroborate that the founder is indeed performing executive level work and they have staff that they supervise. Also, organizational charts will provide a snapshot view of the teams and are useful in the applications.

Job descriptions for the U.S. office: You will have to provide job descriptions for those working at the U.S. office also. Be sure to include the professional duties of everyone who is currently working and positions that will be filled in the near future. In addition, organizational charts will provide a snapshot view of the teams and are useful in the visa applications.

Information about the employee transferring to the U.S.: Lastly, to ensure the individual qualifies for the transfer, we will want to include at least 12 months of work pay stubs as evidence that the employee worked at the foreign office for at least one year. You should also include their resumes and any references, if possible.

Family members

One of the great benefits of the L-1 visa is that the spouse of the visa holder is permitted to work. It used to be that the spouse would have to apply for a work permit (also known as employment authorization document, or EAD). However, spouses of L-1 visa holders, who receive L-2 visa status can now work upon arrival to the U.S. It is known as "incident to status." There is no limit or restriction to where the spouse can work.

Additionally, children will receive L-2 visas. They can freely attend school, but cannot work. I will often get questions from parents about their teenage children to work during summer breaks. The answer is no—L-2 children do not have permission to work.

It is important to note that the L-2 visas of the spouse and children are dependent on the L-1 visa holder—if the L-1 visa holder loses their status, their family members will lose their L-2 status.

Additionally, it is important to note that the U.S. Citizenship and Immigration Services (USCIS) may scrutinize L-1 visa petitions more closely than other visa categories due to concerns about fraud or abuse. This can result in delays or denials of L-1 visa applications.

Overall, while the L-1 visas provide many benefits for multinational companies and their employees, the challenges associated with obtaining and maintaining them require careful planning and preparation. Nevertheless, the L-1 visas are among my favorites for my clients who can qualify, because it allows them to stay in control of their paperwork and destiny.

What's after the L-1 visa?

Talking of destiny, the L-1A (but not L-1B) can lead to legal permanent residence, or a green card through the EB-1C preference category for Multinational Executives and Managers. You can read chapter 18 to learn more.

12

E-2 TREATY INVESTOR VISA

Quick tips:

- You must be from a country that has a treaty with the United States.[1]
- The E-2 visa is great if you are able to invest funds of your own. It will help you get off the ground without relying on a third party to invest in your company.
- If you own more than 50% of the company, consider this visa.

What is the E-2 visa?

The E-2 visa is a non-immigrant visa that allows foreign entrepreneurs, investors, and business owners to enter and work in the United States for a specific period. You must invest in either a new or an existing business. It is designed for individuals who come from countries that have a treaty of commerce and navigation with the United States.

To qualify for an E-2 visa, an individual must have invested a substantial amount of capital in a U.S. business and must be actively involved in its management or operations. The investment must be sufficient to ensure the success of the business, and the individual must demonstrate that they will be able to support themselves and any dependents during their stay in the United States, as well as ensure the business will be successful.

The duration of stay on an E-2 visa can vary depending on the country of origin, but typically ranges from two to five years. E-2 visa holders can apply for extensions of their stay as long as they continue to meet the requirements of the visa.

One advantage of the E-2 visa is that there is no set minimum investment amount, but rather the investment must be substantial in relation to the type of business being established. Additionally, E-2 visa holders are allowed to travel in and out of the United States freely and can bring their spouse and children with them.

What kinds of business investments qualify?

The E-2 visa is essentially an economic development visa. The application process will require evidence that you will invest funds, generate revenue and create jobs for Americans. It can be in any industry as long as you are able to show the business will be profitable (also known as "marginality").

For the modern-day tech entrepreneur, you can use this visa to get a foothold in the U.S. If you own 100% of the company, then that's simple. But if you have multiple co-founders, things get a little challenging. If the nationality of the founders are the same, and you have two founders, then you can likely both apply for an E-2 under the same company. In this situation, you may own 50% each, and both will be able to control the business. If there are three co-founders, then unless you own majority shares, the E-2 would not work if no one meets the 50% or greater investment threshold. Working strategically with both your corporate and immigration lawyer is essential.

The E-2 visa can be used in any industry. You can be selling goods or services. You may buy an existing business or set up a new one. People have used this in the hospitality industry, construction, retail, education, agricultural industry, and so much more. The key is that the business will be profitable

How much to invest?

The law does not specify the amount to be invested in the E-2 visa category. Often people get this visa confused with the EB-5 visa, which is also an investment visa, but it has specific investment minimums for a green card. Don't be confused. The E-2 is for a temporary work visa and the investment must be proportionate to the business. While the law does not state an amount, the rule of thumb is generally about $100,000. Lower amounts can work, but strategize with your lawyer about that. In essence, the capital investment must be substantial and sufficient to start and operate the business.

Preparation guidance:

I tell my clients to focus on five specific categories of documentation.

Active and operating business: The business must be active and operating at the time of filing the case. That means your business entity must be formed. Most tech companies, especially if there are multiple founders and investors, will have articles and certificate of incorporation, state and city licenses and bank account documents. If you are purchasing a coffee shop—like our client did when he paid more than $1 million for a cafe in downtown Seattle—all of the business documentation must be transferred to the buyer's name. Business documents include the state entity forms and certificates, any licenses to operate the business, such as health permits and liquor licenses if you have a restaurant, or a dental license if you own a dental practice, for example. In short, any documentation you need to operate the business will be required first. Other documents will include bank account information, tax identification number and more.

During the Covid-19 pandemic, the policy for requiring an office space was removed. However, I tell everyone that it is better to have an office space. The office space will depend on the type of business you operate. If you have invested in a dance studio, it is reasonable to demonstrate you have a studio space because it is not necessarily reasonable to conduct rehearsals and lessons from your home. Same goes for medical practices. However, for tech companies, remote work is reasonable and possible. Therefore, the nature of your business will determine the best strategy for your case.

Are your funds at risk: The application process will require evidence that your funds are at risk. That means, your funds must have been used to set up or purchase the business. What the adjudicators do not want to see is $100,000 sitting in the business' bank account only to be removed upon receiving the visa. For example, if you are buying a coffee shop, your money will go to the seller, with the aim of making the money back from your new business—but there is a risk. In some cases, to minimize the risk to yourself when you're buying a business, you could request to have the funds in an escrow account to be held until the visa is approved. But most sellers cannot wait too long once the business ownership changes hands. You must work closely with your lawyers for the best strategy for you.

For tech companies, setting up the business doesn't necessarily require much expenses, but you need to show some monetary investment. There are often expenses for office space, so getting a longer lease is part of the investment. You can also count expenses to protect your intellectual property such as patents or trademarks. Your software, and other operational expenditures—all of these costs can be counted as investments in your business.

Your business type will dictate where your startup expenses will go. But it is necessary to spend as part of this exercise.

Source and path of funds: One of the first items to think about in E-2 cases is from where your funds derived. Did you earn the startup capital that you are investing? Are they from savings? Or did your parents give you the funds? No matter how you obtained the money for investment, you must prove the source of the funds. This can be done with bank statements, tax returns, pay stubs or other types of official financial statements. If someone gives you the funds, then the giftor's source of funds will be necessary. Sometimes people sell assets such as real estate or jewelry to raise the money for their investments. You will need evidence of those.

Will your business be profitable? The immigration officers reviewing your application will focus on "marginality." In other words, will the business make suffcient revenue for you to cover your personal expenses, the business operational costs and make a profit.

How do you prove this if your business is brand new, such as a tech startup? If you already have contracts with clients or potential clients, those are excellent items to prove you will be generating revenue from the get-go. But more importantly, you will need a strong business plan which will essentially tell the story of your business, and discuss the projections for revenue and staff growth.

For existing businesses that are sold, such as a restaurant, the tax returns of the existing business will be important to show revenue. Still, in these situations, a business plan is equally important. I suggest you work with a reputable business plan writer who knows immigration laws well to ensure the relevant issues are covered in the plan.

Are you competent to direct and operate your business: Your personal background will be incredibly important for the immigration officer to have faith that you can direct and operate a business. For this, you will need your resume, educational documentation, any certificates and any references from colleagues or clients. It is also important to be able to speak English. Though many businesses may not require English language competence to provide its main services, such as operating a foreign language after-school program, the immigration officers will want to know you can speak and understand at least enough English to operate the business, pay taxes, etc. We have seen many different types of challenges at our office and language competency has come up as an issue.

What about family members?

Your spouse will be able to work in the US upon arrival. Like for the L-1 visa described in chapter 9, E-2 spouses are also entitled to work "incident to status." Therefore, no additional work authorization is required. Spouses can work anywhere they want, there are no restrictions.

Children under 21 can join their parent and live in the U.S. and attend school, but cannot work. Once children reach the age of 21 years old, they have to find their own visa pathway.

Every case will need its own strategy and typically children who turn 21 years old will change to student visas, there may be other options to consider too.

I have a fond memory of a client's son who turned 21 but simply didn't want to attend school and pursue a degree, much to my client's consternation. The son instead wanted to follow in his parents' footsteps in the family business – a UPS shipping franchise. In fact, my client owned multiple franchise locations and the son had basically grown up in these stores. The son, with gifted funds from the father, started a joint business with the mother who had work authorization. We were able to obtain an E-2 for the son.

How much time will an E-2 application take?

The preparation timeline for most E-2 applications can take several months, especially if you are buying an existing business. However, setting up a business, such as a startup, can be much quicker. The preparation timeline will depend on how fast you can generate the above-mentioned documentation.

But once you are ready to apply, your personal circumstances will determine how best to file the application. It is best to file at the U.S. consulate which has the authorization to issue a visa stamp. In my experience, most successful business leaders need to travel internationally and a visa stamp is a prerequisite for reentering the U.S. However, the Covid-19 pandemic created a huge backlog at all U.S. consulates around the world.[2] Though the waiting time has been shrinking, it is important to take consulate timelines into account.

Though typically people file E-2s at the consulate, the pandemic brought a shift and changing status in the U.S. became a reluctant first choice. So, know that it is possible to file the application with USCIS and you can file using premium processing. However, in this situation, even if you receive an approval for your E-2 application in the U.S., you still have to file at the consulate when you travel abroad. What is best for your case will depend on your circumstances.

Who else at my startup can qualify for an E-2 visa?

The E-2 visa is a great option if you intend to scale your business quickly. It is often difficult to find the level of skilled employees you may need to help scale your business. The E-2 allows essential employees to also hold E-2 visas.

What are the risks of growing the business?

The E-2 visa holder must always hold majority shares, at least 50 percent. But as you attract investors to grow your business and your shares dilute, it is important to plan and strategize the visa implications. Your E-2 status could be at risk if you attract enough other investors, to shrink your percentage to less than 50% of the investments—but not having enough money could stall your business' growth or viability. Some of my clients have been able to obtain green cards before such changes occurred, others have obtained O-1 or H-1B visas. Keeping an eye on this issue is paramount.

Can the E-2 lead to a green card?

The path to a green card is not necessarily straightforward from an E-2. There are many E-2 visa holders in the U.S. who have lived and worked here for many decades. Unlike the L-1A or O-1A, which have the EB-1 options, the E-2 doesn't have that. Often people will invest more money into the E-2 business entity so they can qualify for an EB-5 visa, which does lead to a green card. Or, the National Interest Waiver may be a potential option (see chapter 19). Ultimately, your circumstances will dictate your path to a green card.

Final words on the E-2 visa:

E-2 investor visas are one of my favorite visa categories. For those who are eligible, it allows freedom and control over the entire application. You do not have to wait for testimonials in the same way the O visa requires. You don't need a sponsoring employer that H-1B, L-1 or other visas will require. So, even though there are risks and pitfalls, it is a fantastic gateway into the U.S. market for those who have dreamed of opening their businesses here.

13

O-1 EXTRAORDINARY ABILITY VISA

Quick Tips:

- This is for you if you have received some level of "fame" or notability in your industry, particularly if you have raised significant funding.
- Consider this if you have a STEM background.
- If you are an entrepreneur on another visa and need a stepping stone towards a green card, consider these options.

What is the O-1 visa?

The O-1 visa is often referred to as the "genius visa" or the "Einstein visa" because it is designed to attract and retain individuals who have "extraordinary ability" in their field.

It is a non-immigrant visa category for individuals who possess well-recognized expertise in the sciences, arts, education, business, or athletics; or who have a demonstrated record of achievement in the motion picture or television industry, and have been recognized nationally or internationally for those achievements.

The O-1 visa allows the holder to work in the United States for up to three years, with the possibility of extensions.

To be eligible for an O-1 visa, the individual must meet certain criteria and provide evidence of their extraordinary ability or achievement in their field. This evidence can include awards, publications, and testimonials from experts in their field. Additionally, the individual must have a job offer or contract in the United States in their field of expertise. I will discuss these in more detail below.

There are two subcategories of the O-1 visa. The O-1A is reserved for those in the field of science, education, business and athletics. There are eight requirements and you must meet at least three of them. The O-1B is reserved for those in the field of arts. There are six requirements and you must meet at least three. I will focus on guidance for the O-1A below as most startups, founders and entrepreneurs will use this category. But creative artist types who are also entrepreneurs may consider this too.

The O-1 visa does not have a quota or a timeline for filing. In other words, there is no limit to how many O-1 visas that the U.S. can approve in a fiscal year, and people can apply for this visa at any time of year. These features make the O-1 an appealing type of visa for an applicant.

However, there is no doubt that the O-1 visa is complicated and needs a good deal of strategic preparation, both in collating evidence but also in timing the preparation and setting a filing date based on your personal circumstances. It can take a considerable amount of time gathering the evidence, especially reference letters required for this visa category. Therefore, you must plan ahead, and be strategic if you pursue this visa.

O-1A visa for founders and entrepreneurs:

The O-1 is an increasingly important visa for startup founders and entrepreneurs. The H-1B random selection process, otherwise known as the "H-1B lottery" received over 780,000 applications for only 85,000 visas in March 2023 (fiscal year 2024). It is going to be even more difficult for founders to either enter the U.S. market afresh, or to transition from a student visa to a different visa category. If you are a startup founder who does not require a U.S. visa but are looking to scale, trying to hire employees on an H-1B visa will be challenging, and you might want to look at other options that fit your situation. Here are some situations in which you would want to start thinking of an O-1:

- You are a student on your OPT working on your startup.
- You are on an existing H-1B or L-1 visa and were born in India, China, Philippines or Mexico—all places for which the green card waiting time is severely backlogged. Sometimes it can take decades for people from these countries to receive a green card. The temporary O-1A may give you the opportunity to transition to one of the EB-1 permanent visas for people who demonstrate "extraordinary ability" in their fields. That could be a faster path to a green card, though it is by no means automatic.
- If you are working in the U.S. on the International Entrepreneur Parole, you should consider the O-1 as your next step, especially if none of the other visas mentioned in this book are immediately available to you.
- If you are a startup founder looking to scale, and need to hire foreign talent, you may need to keep the O-1 visa at the top of the options list to sponsor your workers.

Reference letters:

For some applicants, the O-1 is a no-brainer. They have already accumulated awards, grants, published articles, press, and general notability through their work and publications. Perhaps they have raised funds as a startup founder, appeared in publications, commanded a high-salary and much more, to meet the eligibility requirements of an O-1. For this group of "geniuses," the bulk of the hard work goes into collating reference letters from people who can attest to their good work. I suggest to my clients to do a self-assessment and think of friends and colleagues who can attest to the O-1 criteria they meet. It is possible that the friend or colleague can attest to multiple visa categories. Crucially, the letter writers must ensure they address the specific O-1 criteria and related issues, and not just praise you generally on your greatness. Therefore, focusing on detailed letters will be one of the most important tasks.

My clients' most frequently asked question regarding reference letters is whether I can provide a sample letter. While I can, and sometimes do, it is much better to follow the below simple format for any declaration that will be used in many types of immigration cases, but especially in the O-1A, EB-1A, and national interest waiver applications. I am copying below what you will have read in chapter 2.

I like to give my clients a simple structure for writing these letters.

There are four components to a winning declaration:

1. Introduction of the author of the declaration: This is where the author must "brag" about themselves. They will essentially summarize their resume, awards, work titles, institutions they have served, etc. This may take one or two paragraphs, that is okay. Brag away!
2. How the author knows the applicant: This is where the author will state how they came to know the applicant, where and when they met and detail first impressions.
3. The author's observation of the applicant's work: The author should detail the observation of the applicant's

work and share experiences of working with them. This is where the author can address as many of the requirements of the O-1/EB-1 to which they are able to attest. I tell my clients to brag about the achievements and talent they have observed.

4. Conclusion: The conclusion of the declaration should include the author's conviction of why the applicant's work and talent is necessary for that industry/product/service and how America benefits from it.

In addition, always include the resume or curriculum vitae of the person writing the declaration. I tell my clients that O-1, EB-1 and NIW are generally "brag fests." Nothing is too small to brag about. The letter writer should brag about their own accomplishments and also brag about the applicant's accomplishments and add their own likely lengthy resume. Ultimately, USCIS is looking to see that one of the top people in the industry is verifying that you, the applicant (or the person you are sponsoring), are also one of the best.

Materials in publications:

Often, many people have the foundations and makings of greatness. I see that in my clients all of the time. But life has not given enough opportunities for them to "brag" yet—either because they are still too young as new graduates, or they have been an employee somewhere for years and have not yet had the chance to shine alone. In these situations, some people have to start building up the O-1A evidential requirements. I suggest to my clients to review each criteria and make a plan on which ones are feasible for them. One way to build up this evidence is to seek publicity of your work and your business.

If you are a startup founder, it would be important to start ensuring your business has a marketing and communications manager, team or person. Marketing is generally used to publicize your products and services, and get them mentioned in the media or recognized in their industry. And that is exactly what you will do—to the benefit of both your company and your ability to demonstrate extraordinary ability. I tell my clients to do all the things you would generally do to market your business, and in that process, as a founder you also will shine. Your communications person, whether internal to your organization or external, can assist placing your company and you in the media. If your startup is focused in a specific industry, chances are there are industry-specific publications. The media placements will help meet one or two O-1 criteria.

Not all publicity is the same. USCIS will want to know where your articles have been published or which publications have featured you. The circulation of those media outlets will be taken into account. For example, being featured or quoted in the New York Times, Wall Street Journal, Forbes, your local American Business Journal, or on broadcast stations such as NPR or NBC, will hold much more credibility than a local newsletter that doesn't have much readership. Make a plan with your communications team on all the criteria including for awards and grants, and start executing the plan as soon as you are able.

Consultation:

Part of the O-1 application process requires that there is a written advisory opinion from a peer group, which can include labor organizations, or a person with expertise in the beneficiary's area of ability. This is called a consultation. If the O-1 petition is for an individual with extraordinary achievement in motion pictures or television, the consultation must come from an appropriate labor union and a management organization with expertise in the beneficiary's area of ability. If a peer group is not available, you can follow the above declaration format to seek a letter from someone with expertise. It does not have to be someone who has worked with you, though it can be. When you are planning your O-1 strategy, this will have to be at the top of your list. If a peer group is not available, who can write this letter for you who has the credibility and expertise in this area?

The Evidence:

I tell all my clients that the immigration forms are a vehicle for USCIS to categorize your case, but it is not the forms that win the case, it is the evidence.

What I tell my clients is that the work you are doing to get your startup off the ground and into a successful company, will help towards your visa application. For an O-1 situation, all your fundraising efforts will be crucially important. The investor you meet may be impressed by you, even if you do not receive funds from them. Consider asking them to write a reference letter for you. Any and all funds will be part of the evidence of an O-1, and they all add up, even if you receive multiple smaller amounts.

USCIS updated its policy manual recently,[1] including making strides in ensuring that the rules for entrepreneurs are updated and easily understandable. The new guidance does give weight to STEM degrees, fund raising, job creation and all the things startups can excel at. The policy manual is a great resource for you as an entrepreneur and you must read it. It's where you'll find more information about the types of evidence you will need. The Biden administration has made an effort to update the O-1 visa policy to help attract and retain STEM graduates.[2]

Kudos to the Biden Administration and their USCIS business immigration policy teams and advisors, including Doug Rand, Senior Advisor to the USCIS Director for these updates.

The law requires that an O-1A petition include evidence that you or the employee you are sponsoring, has received a major internationally recognized award (such as the Nobel Prize) or at least three of the following forms of evidence:

Awards:

- *Documentation of the beneficiary's receipt of nationally or internationally recognized prizes or awards for excellence in the field of endeavor;*
- The USCIS won't necessarily recognize every prestigious award in your field, so you'll have to "peel back at the layers" and include the background information in your application: who/which organization grants the award, how many are granted each year, who are the past recipients.

Membership:

- *Documentation of the beneficiary's membership in associations in the field for which classification is sought, which require outstanding achievements of their members, as judged by recognized national or international experts in their disciplines or fields;*
- Join organizations and associations if you can. Often the bylaws of the organization will list criteria for eligibility. On this item, I suggest to my clients to collect evidence of membership criteria, membership numbers. How do you prove this is a specialized group? Depending on your industry, there are likely numerous professional associations you can join. One example is Forbes which has different elite groups such as Forbes Business Council or Forbes Technology Council.

Press about you:

- *Published material in professional or major trade publications or major media about the beneficiary relating to the beneficiary's work in the field for which classification is sought, which must include the title, date, and author of such published material, and any necessary translation;*

- If you want to use press coverage as part of your evidence, make sure to get coverage in credible media publications with notable circulation in print and online traffic. Hire the right PR teams that have knowledge about the process. It is a bonus if they understand immigration issues.

Judging the work of others:

- *Evidence of the beneficiary's participation on a panel, or individually, as a judge of the work of others in the same or in an allied field of specialization for which classification is sought*;
- Your volunteerism can pay off for this criterion. If you're judging a competition for people in your field, that implies that other professionals trust that you have a certain level of expertise and knowledge. For lawyers, maybe you are judging mooting competitions. If you are a startup founder, maybe you are judging pitch competitions. The key is that "judging" is not your day job. Volunteer and network to create connections and find opportunities for you to participate.

Original contributions to the field:

- *Evidence of the beneficiary's original scientific, scholarly, or business-related contributions of major significance in the field*
- I learn so much from "genius" clients all the time. Some clients have made profound medical discoveries or major technology breakthroughs. Some are using novel methods to solve chronic problems whether in life sciences, technology and other fields. Think about

patents, trademarks, new groundbreaking products, etc.

Your own publications:

- *Evidence of the beneficiary's authorship of scholarly articles in the field, in professional journals, or other major media;*
- If you have enough to say, and have thoughts about changing the world, write about it and have your communications team pitch it for publication. Sometimes, peer-reviewed articles can take years to publish, but there might be other opportunities, such as industry publications and major news media opinion pages, to share your thoughts.

Leading role at an organization:

- *Evidence that the beneficiary has been employed in a critical or essential capacity for organizations and establishments that have a distinguished reputation;*
- For founders, their company's success often can be tied directly to their "extraordinary ability." But even if you are a worker at a big company, you can still demonstrate that your "genius" contributed to your employer's success. Here's where getting references from colleagues, supervisors or others who have witnessed your work will help your application.

High Salary

- *Evidence that the beneficiary has either commanded a high salary, or will command a high salary or other remuneration for services, as evidenced by contracts or other reliable evidence;*

- For this piece of evidence, you need to ensure you are able to compare your salary to others in the field and demonstrate your salary has been consistently higher than the median. I've always used the Department of Labor website that dictates minimum salaries for H-1B visas. There are other crowd-sourced websites such as Glassdoor that have this information as well. Produce your contracts, offer letters, paystubs, tax returns and anything else you may have to prove the high salary.

Catch-all bucket (comparable evidence):

Sometimes, your evidence won't necessarily fall neatly into one of the above categories. But that doesn't mean you cannot put forward other achievements. The goal is to prove your sustained success in the field. So, think about everything in your life that has gotten you to this point. Nothing is too small. The law does allow for you to submit "comparable" evidence.

O-1B requirements:

I include the O-1B requirements here in case any of you reading this are artists and creatives in any medium. Follow the general guidance above for documentation gathering. You can also visit the USCIS website for more information.

The supporting documentation for an O-1B (Arts) petition must include evidence that the beneficiary has received, or been nominated for, a significant national or international award or prize in the particular field (such as an Academy Award, Emmy, Grammy, or Director's Guild Award) or at least three of the following forms of evidence.

- Evidence that the beneficiary has performed, and will perform, services as a lead or starring participant in productions or events that have a distinguished reputation, as evidenced by critical reviews, advertisements, publicity releases, publications, contracts, or endorsements;

- Evidence that the beneficiary has achieved national or international recognition for achievements, as evidenced by critical reviews or other published materials, by or about the beneficiary, in major newspapers, trade journals, magazines, or other publications;
- Evidence that the beneficiary has performed, and will perform, in a lead, starring, or critical role for organizations and establishments that have a distinguished reputation, as evidenced by articles in newspapers, trade journals, publications, or testimonials;
- Evidence that the beneficiary has a record of major commercial or critically acclaimed successes, as evidenced by such indicators as title, rating, standing in the field, box office receipts, motion pictures or television ratings, and other occupational achievements reported in trade journals, major newspapers, or other publications;
- Evidence that the beneficiary has received significant recognition for achievements from organizations, critics, government agencies, or other recognized experts in the field in which the beneficiary is engaged. Such testimonials must be in a form which clearly indicates the author's authority, expertise, and knowledge of the beneficiary's achievements; or
- Evidence that the beneficiary has either commanded a high salary or will command a high salary or other substantial remuneration for services in relation to others in the field, as evidenced by contracts or other reliable evidence.

Spouse and childrem:

The O-1 visa holders' spouses and children under 21 years of age, can reside in the U.S. with an O-3 visa. Unlike people with other spouse visas, an O-3 visa holder is not permitted to work.

What's after the O visa?

Once you have successfully obtained the O-1 visa, whether for yourself as the founder or for your employee, it would be important to think about the next step on this immigration journey. That is generally, the green card. The EB-1A is a natural next step for O-1 visa holders. All the preparation you have read above will apply to the EB-1A. You can learn more at Chapter 16.

14

OTHER NON-IMMIGRANT VISAS

I've covered the most used visas for startups and founders in individual chapters. Here I will briefly mention other visas so you can be aware of them. These visas may be better suited for your startup employees rather than founders, but they can be used for founders in the right circumstances with the right strategic preparation.

H-1B1 visa:

The H-1B1 visa is reserved for citizens of Singapore and Chile. From an evidence perspective, the preparation is similar to the regular H-1B (chapter 9). However, these applications are generally filed at the U.S. consulates in those countries. There is an annual limit of 1,400 visas for those from Chile and 5,400 visas for citizens of Singapore. The H-1B1 program is governed by many of the rules that apply to the H-1B program. The period of employment is one year. Extensions may be obtained twice, but only in one-year increments. Further extensions can be obtained only with the filing of a new Labor Condition Application. While this is a limited period of time, at least for startup companies, it could meet a short-term need, or be an entry point for such employees, as the company ramps up.

E-3 visa:

The E-3 visa is specifically for citizens of Australia. The evidential requirements and preparation are similar to the H-1B, discussed at chapter 9. This application can be filed at the consulates in Australia or in the U.S. to extend or change status. Recently, premium processing has been allowed for these types of cases too. It is issued for two years at a time. There is a 10,500 cap each year.

TN visa:

The Treaty NAFTA visa, or TN visa, is specifically for citizens from Canada and Mexico. The NAFTA treaty has an exhaustive list of professions. You must be working in one of those professions and in most cases must hold a degree in that field. If you do not hold a degree, a TN visa is not impossible, but can be challenging. The TN visa is issued for three years at a time. There is no limit to how long you can have the TN visa, unlike the H1-B and other visas which have a maximum time limit.

The TN visa regulations require that you cannot be self-employed, therefore the application must be sponsored by an employer. If the employing company is owned more than 50 percent by the applicant, then that will be considered as self-employment. But because most startups have multiple founders, founders shouldn't immediately rule out considering a TN visa if the other conditions apply. Even if you are a part-owner of your company, if you own less than 50 percent, I think it might be worth considering applying for a TN—making sure all the employer-employee relationship items are addressed in the application. Talk to your lawyer to strategize.

For a startup company, the TN visa is a great opportunity. It can be relatively quick to process. Canadians can go to the U.S. border at a port of entry to apply. Mexican citizens can apply at the consulates. These applications can also be filed with the USCIS using Form I-129.

B-1 visa:

The B-1 visa is a great visa – if you can secure it. This is a temporary solution to visit the U.S. for meetings with clients, investors and other business colleagues. You can also set up an office, attend conferences, and even attend accelerator or incubator programs which are important for startup founders.

You will need to prove you are employed abroad, have sufficient ties abroad that you will not stay permanently in the U.S., and have sufficient funds for the expenses you will incur during your trip. You will need to credibly prove you will not receive any form of payment in the U.S. If the consular officers suspect you intend to live or work in the U.S., your application will be denied.

If your application is denied, you are allowed to file again, but ensure you address the concerns in your next application. You will apply for this visa at the consulate directly. Covid-19 backlogs continue to this date and every consulate has a different waiting time. Planning ahead will become an important strategy for anyone trying to obtain a B-1 visa in a post-pandemic era.

J-1/H-3 visas:

If you are a founder coming to the United States to participate in an accelerator or incubator program, these two temporary visas could be options. I tell my clients that these are two sides of the same training coin, so to speak. Both require you to prove you will receive training. The H-3 is filed and adjudicated by USCIS, and the J-1 visa is administered by the Department of State. The organizations that will provide the training or incubation have to file the cases on your behalf. I file a fair number of H-3 visas for those who are training in the U.S. It is not easy but worth exploring and keeping in your toolbox. But in general, it's not a visa for founders generally to rely on for running their companies in the long term.

IMMIGRANT VISAS

15

IMMIGRANT VISA BASICS

Once you have received your temporary work visa, and the startup is becoming successful, your investors and customers will need you to be secure and stable in your status in the U.S. Whether you are on the O-1, H-1B, L-1, or any other visa, it will become apparent that a green card will help everyone focus on the business and not be concerned or distracted by immigration issues, or worse, that the founder may have to leave the U.S. due to immigration problems. Therefore, an immigrant visa becomes the next important focus.

In Chapter 3, I described that an immigrant visa, commonly called a "green card," allows a person to live in the U.S. permanently. The U.S. immigrant visa system has two broad overarching categories—employment-based and family-based visas. Each is divided into further sub-categories, generally referred to as "preference categories." There are five employment-based preference categories – EB-1, EB-2, EB-3, EB-4 and EB-5. In the following pages, I will outline the basics of these immigrant visas to quickly identify which might be the path for you.

Side note—during the various startup visa bills that were proposed over the years, a startup immigrant visa was going to be categorized as EB-6, but that never happened. In recent times, a handful of lawyers have misinterpreted or misused the term, confusing it with the International Entrepreneur Rules. Don't be duped! There is no EB-6 visa, yet.

Priority Dates:

This is a good place to explain how you secure a spot in the so-called "line" of 140,000 employment-based green cards a year. The year starts on October 1st which is the fiscal year in the U.S. There is a 7 percent per-country limit of the annual total number of 140,000. That means citizens from countries with higher populations generally have to wait longer. Each of the preference categories I mention above, has a limited number of immigrant visas available each year. As a result, there are backlogs that have built up for most of the categories.

In the context of U.S. immigration law, a priority date refers to the date when a petition or application is filed with USCIS. The priority date is significant because it determines your place in line for the allocation of an immigrant visa. The priority date can be found on the approval notice or receipt notice issued by the USCIS.

Every month, the Department of State publishes the Visa Bulletin,[1] which provides monthly updates on the availability of immigrant visas based on priority dates and visa quotas. If your priority date is listed, that means that your priority date has become current, and you can move to your next steps in the immigration process.

"Current" means that your place in the line is now at the front and your waiting time is over. It means that the final steps of the green card application can proceed. However, most applicants have a long wait until their priority date becomes current.

It's important to note that the priority date will vary based on the specific immigration category and the applicant's country of origin, and certain countries have higher demand for immigrant visas resulting in longer waiting times. People born in India, mainland China, Philippines and Mexico in general, have a longer waiting time because those countries have high numbers of people who are applying for the limited quota of green cards.

Additionally, approved Form I-140 employment-based priority dates may be used between EB-1, EB-2 and EB-3. For example, if you have an approved I-140 and a priority date in the EB-3 (skilled worker) preference category, you can use that priority date for an EB-1A (extraordinary ability) that you might file. In the startup context, that can be advantageous.

As an example, Ms. Piggy was born in China and holds a bachelor's degree. She has worked as a software engineer at Company Big Tech A for twelve years on an H-1B (specialty occupation). Big Tech A filed her immigrant visa and she now has a priority date of January 2014. But some years later, she started the New Sesame Revolution company which is working on cutting edge technology. She has an H-1B for her startup (see chapter 9) but because of her ownership in the company, she cannot file a PERM (permanent worker, see chapter 22). However, she could possibly file a National Interest Waiver (see chapter 19) or an EB-1A (chapter 16). She could use her 2014 priority date for her new application, and likely be able to get a green card faster because the waiting time may likely be shorter in the other categories. This is why having an immigration strategy based on your startup from the very beginning is imperative.

Preparation:

Read Chapter 2 for preparation of evidence for these visas. Additionally, read chapter 13 on the O-1. All the actions you will learn to take in those chapters will help prepare your EB-1A, EB-1B and National Interest Waiver immigrant visa applications—whether it is for you as the founder, or for an employee.

Summary:

Green card applications are part and parcel of the U.S. immigration journey for those who want to live and work here permanently. The path can be long, tedious and complicated. Sometimes we may have multiple non-immigrant visas before we can get to the most appropriate green card option for you. I would strongly recommend you read my article from *Above the Law - The Immigration Journey of an Entrepreneur*[2] reprinted at the back of this book with permission from the publication.

With perseverance, determination and teamwork, you can get to the finish line and be a legal permanent resident—aka, a green card holder—in the U.S.

16

EB-1A EXTRAORDINARY ABILITY

Quick Tips:

- You do not need an employer to sponsor you.
- If you have secured an O-1A, then plan your EB-1A without too much delay.
- You may consider an EB-1A while you hold other visas such as an H-1B visa.
- EB-1A applications can be filed using premium processing and can provide some strategic advantage if you are running out of non-immigrant visa time.

What is the EB-1A visa?

The EB-1A visa, also known as the Employment-Based First Preference visa, is a type of visa that allows individuals with extraordinary ability in their field to obtain permanent residency in the United States. This visa category is designed for individuals who have reached the very top of their respective fields, such as the sciences, arts, education, business, or athletics, and who can demonstrate exceptional ability in their field through sustained national or international acclaim.

One of the benefits of the EB-1A, especially for startup founders, is you can self-petition, or your startup can sponsor you.

While many people have an O-1 visa before applying for an EB-1, it's not a prerequisite. In recent years, many H-1B visa holders who were born in India or China, either got laid off or stuck in the green card backlog, have applied for the EB-1A—and some have succeeded.

Sometimes, people apply for the EB-1 from their home countries and enter the U.S. directly as an immigrant. The immigrant visa can be independent of your current location, in or outside the U.S.

The EB-1A requirements are similar to the O-1A, though not exactly the same. If you have applied for the O-1 and you are ready to take a look at the EB-1A as an option, it is important to review your O-1 filing if you filed one with an eye for the following: how long ago you obtained some of the evidence, if you have achieved new accolades since you filed the O-1A, and if you can gather additional reference letters. More is more in my opinion!

Additionally, it is important to keep in mind that if you do hold a successful O-1A, it doesn't necessarily mean you will be successful in the EB-1A application. The decision standard is a little different. Not only do you have to meet at least three of the EB-1 requirements, there is a further "merits test" as an overall judgment about whether you are indeed extraordinary.

The merits test was set by a case titled *Matter of Kazarian.*[1] This case essentially set a two-part process for deciding EB-1A cases. First the immigration officers must decide whether you do indeed meet at least three of the ten requirements detailed below. And if they believe you do, then the officers make an objective decision, based on all the evidence as to whether you are indeed extraordinary.

The EB-1 is something you should strongly consider if you were born in India and China, as those born in these countries generally wait for decades before obtaining their green cards. EB-1 can give them a shorter waiting time. Therefore, should you decide to file the O-1, do it with the intention to file an EB-1 and prepare accordingly.

The EB-1A requirements:

Similar to an O-1, you can include evidence of a one-time achievement—that is, a major, international recognized award—or at least three of the following ten requirements:

1. Evidence of receipt of lesser nationally or internationally recognized prizes or awards for excellence;
2. Evidence of your membership in associations in the field which demand outstanding achievement of their members;
3. Evidence of published material about you in professional or major trade publications or other major media;
4. Evidence that you have been asked to judge the work of others, either individually or on a panel;
5. Evidence of your original scientific, scholarly, artistic, athletic, or business-related contributions of major significance to the field;
6. Evidence of your authorship of scholarly articles in professional or major trade publications or other major media;
7. Evidence that your work has been displayed at artistic exhibitions or showcases;
8. Evidence of your performance of a leading or critical role in distinguished organizations;
9. Evidence that you command a high salary or other significantly high remuneration in relation to others in the field; or
10. Evidence of your commercial successes in the performing arts.

And if there are achievements that you can list that do not readily fall into one of the above categories, you can include them in a "comparable" category, which I explain in the chapter on the O-1A.

Preparation:

Many parts of preparing for the EB-1A are very similar to applying for the O-1A—with a few exceptions that I will describe below. Read chapter 2 regarding general preparation for applying for visas and read chapter 13 on the O-1. All of that information will be the foundation for preparing your EB-1A application.

The Final Merits Test:

The final merits test is essentially an overall analysis as to whether the applicant is indeed extraordinary. The officer should evaluate the evidence together and consider the petition in its entirety, to make a final merits determination of whether or not the petitioner—whether that's the sponsoring employer or it is being self-sponsored—has demonstrated that the person has sustained national or international acclaim and that his or her achievements have been recognized in the field of expertise. The immigration official is looking for evidence that this person is one of that small percentage who has risen to the very top of their field of endeavor. The officer will decide, whether on balance, whether extraordinary ability has been proven.

For this analysis, it is important that you put forward why all the evidence makes you extraordinary. In other words, once you have presented the evidence, you will need to explain why all of the evidence together makes you one of the best in your industry.

17

EB-1B OUTSTANDING PROFESSOR OR RESEARCHER

Quick Tips:

- Startup employers should consider this as an option to sponsor employees who focus on research and development as an "outstanding researcher."
- You must have an employer, this cannot be self-petitioned.
- Premium processing is not available for this preference category.

What is the EB-1B preference category?

Though the EB-1B is used primarily in the academic field, it can be a useful category for startups to consider for employees with advanced degrees working in research and development.

This preference category requires that you prove international recognition for your outstanding achievements in a particular academic field. You must have at least three years of experience in researching or teaching in that academic area. In general, you must be entering the U.S. to pursue tenure, a tenure track teaching, or comparable research position at a university or other institution of higher education. You must also have a job offer from a university, institution of higher learning, or department, division or an institute of a private employer.

When it comes to a private employer, the position must be in the employee's academic field. The department, division, or institute must prove that it employs at least three persons full-time in research positions, and that it has achieved documented accomplishments in an academic field.

In the startup context, this could be an option for those of you who are in research and development (R&D). There are many companies that focus on research and development, either as part of their work or with an R&D arm. Often companies employ those with a Master's degree or higher in the STEM fields for these positions.

In my opinion, with the Chips and Science Act passed recently, technology research and development will become even more important, especially as the U.S. government will have financial incentives for companies focusing on relevant issues. One of the things that the Chips and Science Act does, is to establish a new directorate within the National Science Foundation to accelerate commercialization of critical technologies in the United States such as energy, artificial intelligence, quantum computing, and advanced manufacturing. This is a unique moment in history, I believe, for considering this category in creative ways.

What are the requirements of EB-1B Outstanding Professor or Researcher?

In order to demonstrate you are an outstanding researcher—as a private employer would file—you must include evidence of two of the six listed criteria below (or comparable evidence if any of the criteria do not readily apply):

1. Evidence of receipt of major prizes or awards for outstanding achievement;
2. Evidence of membership in associations that require their members to demonstrate outstanding achievement;
3. Evidence of published material in professional publications written by others about the noncitizen's work in the academic field;
4. Evidence of participation, either on a panel or individually, as a judge of the work of others in the same or allied academic field;
5. Evidence of original scientific or scholarly research contributions in the field;
6. Evidence of authorship of scholarly books or articles (in scholarly journals with international circulation) in the field.

As you can see, the required items are less burdensome than the EB-1A or even the National Interest Waiver. The key is that an employer must file this application.

Preparation:

Many, but not all, of the requirements are similar to those of the O-1 visa. For more advice about how to prove your merit for the EB-1B visa, read chapter 2 on general preparation tips and chapter 13 on O-1 visa for guidance on document gathering and preparation strategy.

In summary, this category is a good option to keep in the startup immigration toolbox.

18

EB-1C MULTINATIONAL EXECUTIVE OR MANAGER

Quick tips:

- When you are on an L-1A visa, EB-1C will likely be the path to permanent residence.
- The U.S. entity must be at least one year old before you can consider an EB-1C.
- You can apply for an EB-1C immigrant visa without holding an L-1A first.
- You can now file the EB-1C Form I-140 using premium processing.

The category of the application is EB-1C, Employment-based First Preference category for Multinational Executives and Managers. For some in the United States under an L-1A visa (but not the L-1B), the EB-1C can lead to legal permanent residence in the U.S. The requirements are similar to that of an L-1A discussed in Chapter 11, with the exception that the U.S. entity must have been operating for at least one year. But you don't need to have an L-1A as a prerequisite to the EB-1C.

When should you apply?

This will depend on the facts of your case, including the employer's year-to-year growth in revenue and employees, the age of your children and your future goals, such as whether you want to live in the U.S. permanently. While for many, living permanently in the U.S. is the dream, there are also many people who plan to return to their home countries, or want to explore life in another country after their time in the United States. Work closely with your immigration lawyer.

Requirements:

- The company must be a U.S. employer with a qualifying relationship with a foreign company, such as a parent company, branch, subsidiary, or affiliate. These are collectively referred to as "qualifying entities."
- The company must operate in the U.S. and in at least one other country, either directly or through a qualifying entity, in the regular, systematic, and continuous provision of goods or services.
- The company must have been conducting business in the U.S. for at least one year prior to filing.
- The person who is seeking permanent residency must have been employed in a managerial or executive capacity by the overseas affiliate, parent, subsidiary or branch of the U.S. employer for at least one of the three years prior to filing the petition.
- They must also intend to immigrate to the U.S. to work in a managerial or executive capacity with the employer. Additional conditions apply according to the professional capacity an alien is seeking to assume.
- Managerial evidence includes that the primary duties include:

1. Manages the organization, department, component, or function;
2. Supervises and controls the work of other supervisory, professional, or managerial employees, or manages an essential function within the organization, or a department or subdivision of the organization;
3. Has the authority to hire, terminate, and make other personnel decisions; and
4. Exercises discretion over day-to-day operations of the activity or function.

- Executive duties mean that the person primarily:

1. Directs the management of an organization, major component, or function;
2. Establishes goals and policies;
3. Exercises wide latitude in discretionary decision-making; and
4. Receives only general supervision from higher executives, the board of directors, or stockholders.

Preparation:

Please read chapter 11 on L-1 visas so you can read detailed guidance on preparation of the EB-1C. In essence, if you have already filed an L-1A application, you can update the filing with the latest financial to prove your company has been on track for growth. You can add updated organizational charts to prove staff growth and your position in the company. The USCIS adjudicators are looking for high-level decision makers whose primary duties are executive in nature or managerial. In these types of cases, often the most significant scrutiny is on the job description.

In sum, similar to the L-1A, I like the EB-1C for my clients. The more successful you are, the stronger your application will be.

19

EB-2 NATIONAL INTEREST WAIVER

Quick Tips:

- You can self-sponsor, meaning you do not need an employer to sponsor your green card.
- Consider this if you are a founder or entrepreneur and if you do not meet the requirements of an EB-1.
- Consider this if you are a startup company trying to sponsor an employee and want to bypass the costs and trouble of a labor certification.
- Especially consider this as one of your top green card options if you are a founder and were born in a country with a shorter green card waiting time.

What is the National Interest Waiver visa?

The National Interest Waiver (NIW) is a type of employment-based visa in the United States that allows foreign nationals with exceptional abilities or advanced degrees, to apply for a green card (permanent residency) without having to go through the traditional labor certification process.

In other words, the NIW is a way for highly skilled individuals to bypass the traditional employment-based green card process by showing that their work is so important that the United States would benefit from their presence, even without a specific job offer. It is an important option for startup founders and entrepreneurs as it is one of two immigrant visas that can be self-petitioned, and applicants do not need an employer to sponsor them.

This visa is generally referred to as EB-2 NIW. This is because it is the second preference out of the five in the United States' employment-based preference categories.

To qualify for an NIW, an applicant must demonstrate that their work is in the national interest of the U.S., meaning that it has substantial merit and national importance, and that they are well-positioned to advance that work. The applicant must also demonstrate that it would be in the best interest of the U.S. to waive the usual job offer and labor certification requirements.

Why is the NIW important for startup founders and entrepreneurs?

It helps to understand a little history. In 2010, a policy known as the "Neufeld Memo" made it more of a challenge for founders to obtain their H-1Bs. The 2010 policy required applicants to prove the employer-employee relationship in a way that was not previously necessary. In 2012, USCIS established a new policy to allow founders and sole proprietors to obtain the H-1B. But at the same time, it became clear that by virtue of having ownership in their companies, founders would not be able to apply for the labor certification required for the H-1B, because a good faith recruitment to fill the position of "founder" is inherently impossible. The Obama administration tried to fix this by providing policy guidance that founders and entrepreneurs may utilize the National Interest Waiver category for green cards.

However, at the time, the requirements for a National Interest Waiver were onerous and difficult to meet.[1] Therefore, it was not necessarily an effective solution. But in January 2017, the case of *Matter of Dhanasar*[2] created the new legal framework that I mentioned above—that the work has substantive merit, is national in scope and the applicant's work must be beneficial to the U.S. While the new framework applied to all types of applications, it was especially beneficial for entrepreneurs, since they could self-petition and prove all elements, making it a viable option.

In 2023, the Biden administration updated the USCIS policy manual with new detailed guidelines. And now, the National Interest Waiver is something every founder should consider.

Eligibility for National Interest Waiver:

There are two ways to be eligible for a NIW application:

One way is to hold a Master's degree or higher (referred to as an "advanced degree") or to have the "equivalent" to advanced degree, which is generally a Bachelor's degree, PLUS five years of progressive work experience. If you choose to provide evidence of progressive experience, be sure to collate sufficient letters from supervisors or colleagues to show how your career has progressed and developed. Merely confirming that you worked somewhere is not always sufficient.

The second way to qualify if you do not hold an advanced degree or the equivalent, is to show that you have "exceptional ability." Exceptional ability requires you to prove that you meet at least three of the six following types of evidence:

- An official academic record showing that the beneficiary has a degree, diploma, certificate, or similar award from a college, university, school, or other institution of learning relating to the area of exceptional ability;

- Evidence in the form of letter(s) from current or former employer(s) showing that the beneficiary has at least 10 years of full-time experience in the occupation in which he or she is being sought;
- A license to practice the profession or certification for a particular profession or occupation;
- Evidence that the beneficiary has commanded a salary or other remuneration for services that demonstrates exceptional ability. (To satisfy this criterion, the evidence must show that the beneficiary has commanded a salary or remuneration for services that is indicative of his or her claimed exceptional ability relative to others working in the field);
- Evidence of membership in professional associations; and
- Evidence of recognition for achievements and significant contributions to the industry or field by peers, governmental entities, or professional or business organizations.

Proving the three prongs of the National Interest Waiver:

What I tell all my clients is that each case is a story. This is no different. Making a case that you qualify for the National Interest Waiver is the story of you, a compilation of your career highlights, documented and corroborated by evidence of education, achievements, testimonials from colleagues, and much more. No evidence is too small to discuss with your lawyer.

There are three prongs of this visa that you will have to demonstrate

1. That the applicant's proposed endeavor (in their field of study) has an important impact in the United States. The impact does not have to be quantifiable initially. The impact can also be regional/local in nature.

2. That the applicant is well-positioned, based on their credentials and experience, to carry out the proposed endeavor.
3. That it would be beneficial for the United States to waive the DOL certification of recruitment.

I will break down how you will make the case for each prong.

First Prong: The Proposed Endeavor has both Substantial Merit and National Importance

Endeavor: In essence, explain what your job is and what kind of work you will be doing.

Substantive merit: You must prove that your job requires significant skills. You can prove the endeavor's merit in any industry including, but not limited to, business, entrepreneurship, science, technology, culture, health, or education. It could be an economic impact such as creating jobs, or it could be the impact on human knowledge, such as making scientific breakthroughs. Think about your story and what makes your story compelling.

When it comes to national importance, the work doesn't necessarily have to have a wide geographic presence, though it certainly helps! You need to show how your venture will have potential national impact. For example, your work might address the housing crisis, or climate change. Do you have the potential to advance technology, cultural, or social welfare issues? Document everything you can to tell the story of your business and the profound impact it will make, and why it is of national importance.

Second Prong: The Person is Well Positioned to Advance the Proposed Endeavor

Unlike the first prong, which focuses on the merit and importance of the proposed endeavor, the second prong centers on the person. Specifically, you must prove that you are well positioned to advance the endeavor. USCIS has provided the following sample list of ways to prove it:

- The person's education, skills, knowledge, and record of success in related or similar efforts;
- A model or plan that the person developed, or played a significant role in developing, for future activities related to the proposed endeavor;
- Any progress towards achieving the proposed endeavor; and
- The interest or support garnered by the person from potential customers, users, investors, or other relevant entities or persons.

I often tell my clients to do a self-assessment on the O-1 visa since it is an easier way to create structure for this exercise. All the evidence and items that you can collate can be used for a NIW. It's important to note that we don't have to prove you will succeed in your plans. We only need to prove you are in a position to push your plans forward. USCIS has provided the following list of examples in its guidance:

- Degrees, certificates, or licenses in the field;
- Patents, trademarks, or copyrights developed by the person;
- Letters from experts in the person's field, describing the person's past achievements and providing specific examples of how the person is well positioned to advance the person's endeavor;
- Published articles or media reports about the person's achievements or current work;
- Documentation demonstrating a strong citation history of the person's work or excerpts of published articles

showing positive discourse around, or adoption of, the person's work;

- Evidence that the person's work has influenced the field of endeavor;
- A plan describing how the person intends to continue the proposed work in the United States;
- A detailed business plan or other description, along with any relevant supporting evidence, when appropriate;
- Correspondence from prospective or potential employers, clients, or customers;
- Documentation reflecting feasible plans for financial support;
- Evidence that the person has received investment from U.S. investors, such as venture capital firms, angel investors, or startup accelerators, and that the amounts are appropriate to the relevant endeavor;
- Copies of contracts, agreements, or licenses showing the potential impact of the proposed endeavor;
- Letters from government agencies or quasi-governmental entities in the United States demonstrating that the person is well positioned to advance the proposed endeavor;
- Evidence that the person has received awards or grants or other indications of relevant non-monetary support (for example, using facilities free of charge) from federal, state, or local government entities with expertise in economic development, research and development, or job creation; and
- Evidence demonstrating how the person's work is being used by others, such as, but not limited to:
- Contracts with companies using products that the person developed or assisted in developing;
- Documents showing technology that the person invented, or contributed to inventing, and how others use that technology; and

- Patents or licenses for innovations the person developed with documentation showing why the patent or license is significant to the field.

Third Prong: On balance, it would be beneficial to the United States to waive the job offer and thus the permanent labor certification requirements

The third prong is essentially proving why there wouldn't be someone like you to do this job. National Interest Waiver means you are "waiving" the requirement to make a good faith effort to recruit an American worker (see chapter 22). In this case, you are requesting that immigration officials waive the requirement for a recruitment effort for your job, because of you and your nationally important work.

So, an immigration officer will assess whether all the evidence taken as a whole, proves you and your work, will be in the interest of the nation—are you solving national problems, creating jobs, growing your revenue etc. As such, you also need to provide evidence to prove the following.

- The impracticality of a labor certification application;
- The benefit to the United States from the prospective noncitizen's contributions, even if other U.S. workers were also available; and
- The national interest in the person's contributions is sufficiently urgent, such as U.S. competitiveness in STEM fields.
- Whether urgency, such as public health or safety, warrants foregoing the labor certification process;
- Whether the labor certification process may prevent an employer from hiring a person with unique knowledge or skills exceeding the minimum requirements standard for that occupation, which cannot be appropriately captured by the labor certification;

- Whether the person's endeavor has the potential to generate considerable revenue consistent, for example, with economic revitalization; and
- Whether the person's endeavor may lead to potential job creation.

Note that evidence can overlap in all three prongs and you can repeat the evidence and discuss them from different perspectives. Think about your strengths, what makes you uniquely you, why you can envision something that others cannot and tell the story of you and your vision.

Other considerations and benefits:

Sometimes there are those (whether you are the founder or sponsoring your employee), who have worked at multinational companies where the employer filed a PERM for them (see chapter 22). The approval allowed the person to enter the "line" or have "priority date" for receiving the green card (see chapter 15). For those born in India and China, that is a really long waiting time. But if you switch to a NIW application by virtue of creating a startup, you are able to keep your spot in the line and possibly move quicker toward the green card.

Additionally, the Biden administration recently created new policy updates to be able to file your NIW application and receive a result faster. This is generally referred to as premium processing. Though this category has existed for years, premium processing only became available in 2023. It is a huge benefit for my clients and I would strongly recommend you take advantage of it. If you are on an H-1B visa, the 140 approval of the NIW will allow your spouse to receive work permission.

Summary:

For startups, founders and entrepreneurs, the NIW category is a fantastic opportunity, especially if you cannot quite meet the EB-

1A requirements. There's the flexibility of telling your story as you are. And if you are hoping to change the world, revolutionize a new industry, create jobs, raise funds and more, here's your chance to make your case in a way that you can shine.

20

EB-2, EB-3, AND EB-4 PREFERENCE CATEGORIES

Quick tips:

- You generally must have permanent labor certification (PERM) approved for these categories (except the EB-2 National Interest Waiver).
- The following categories are too complex to explain in detail, but I'm including them in this guidebook so readers get a complete picture of all the employment-based preference immigration categories.
- You must talk to your lawyer if any of these apply to you.

EB-2 Advanced Degree or exceptional Ability:

This category is generally for those with a Master's degree or higher. There are nuances of course, but I will not go into those details for the purposes of this book. Typically an employer will file a Permanent Labor Certification (PERM) as the first step and then file a Form I-140. Read Chapter 22 for PERMS.

This option is available to startup employees with Master's degrees, but not generally for founders. One of the requirements is to prove a good-faith effort to recruit an American worker for the person's position—which is not applicable to the founder's role as owner or part-owner of a company.

But if the founder has a previously approved I-140 in this category after working at another company, the founder could use that priority date to advance an EB-1 or National Interest Waiver application.

EB-2 National Interest Waiver:

This is a great option for founders and possibly startup employees. Ownership is not a barrier at all, and in fact, USCIS has policy updates so that founders can meet this category. Read chapter 19 for an in-depth discussion of who might be able to qualify under this category.

EB-3 Skilled, Professional or "Other" Worker:

This option generally is considered for startup employees, but it's not generally available to founders. Similar to what I said above, ownership in the company will be a barrier to proving a good-faith effort to recruit American workers.

However, if a founder has an approved Form I-140 under the EB-3 preference category filed by a previous employer, that priority date can be used for an EB-1 or National Interest Waiver. For example, let's say a person came to the U.S. to work at Microsoft, and they obtained an approved I-140 in 2014 under EB-3. When they leave Microsoft to found their own company, they can file their own National Interest Waiver in 2023 and ask to retain the 2014 priority date, which would keep their immigration case moving along, instead of having to restart at the back of the line.

EB-4 Special Immigrants:

For the sake of including all the EB subgroups in this book, I'll give a brief description of EB-4, which won't apply to most startup founders and employers. The EB-4 visa is reserved for those who are considered "special immigrants." The people who qualify include religious workers, Amerasians,[1] widowers, Afghan nationals and Iraqi nationals, and other subcategories. It is not relevant for startups.

21

EB-5 IMMIGRANT INVESTOR PROGRAM

Quick tips

- A good option for E-2 entrepreneurs to consider if an EB-1 or National Interest Waiver do not seem feasible.
- The immigrant investor's own money must be at risk, therefore, this visa is not for the typical startup founder who is relying solely on funding from external sources to start their company.
- The adjustment of status can be filed together with the EB-5 application making it a more viable option for many, especially those who were either laid off or tired of the backlog.

What is the EB-5 visa?

The EB-5 visa program provides a green card for those investing at least $1,050,000 or $800,000 in a for-profit business that was established after 1990, that promises to create 10 American jobs. In general, this money has to be at the risk of the investor.

The EB-5 visa program can be a great option for those who have the funds. This visa also can be used in all industries. Some of our E-2 entrepreneurs clients have taken this path.

This is a popular visa program for those who invest to immigrate to the U.S. Typically, these investors are high-net worth individuals, and not a founder looking to innovate with venture funding or angel investors.

However, it can be a pathway to a green card for those who have already invested funds in their own startups and have the opportunity to invest more. Read the chapter on E-2 visas (chapter 12) for more information on this option.

Unlike the above visa categories, the EB-5 application is filed using Form I-526 and you cannot interchange the priority dates from an approved I-140.

It might be an option for some of you if you have about a million dollars to spare and you need to strategize an alternative path to a green card. Sometimes people will consider it because the other immigrant visa categories are not suitable, or the waiting time is too long. Sometimes people will consider it because their children will soon be over 21 years old and age out of their existing visas.

Sometimes people will keep working at their day jobs on their non-immigrant visas and use their investment portfolio to keep the EB-5 as a concurrent green card path. You need not be working at the EB-5 investment vehicle company to consider the EB-5 program.

The EB-5 visa category is complicated. Speak to a lawyer if you want to consider this further.

22

PERMANENT LABOR CERTIFICATIONS

Quick Tips:

- If you are a founder, co-founder, owner, related to the owner, and you hope to get a green card for yourself, this chapter is not for you.
- If you are the founder and are hoping to sponsor your employees for a green card, this is for you.
- Be prepared that this will be expensive, time consuming to prepare and process, and depending on the application category and place of birth of the employee, this may take years. But it is likely the only way to sponsor many of the employees who you may want to support.

What is a permanent labor certification?

A Permanent Labor Certification, also known as PERM, is a process that allows U.S. employers to hire foreign workers to work permanently in the United States. It is the employer that applies for PERM, and it paves the way for the company to sponsor a worker's green card.

Before hiring a foreign worker permanently, an employer must demonstrate to the U.S. Department of Labor (DOL) that there are no qualified U.S. workers available for the job and that hiring the foreign worker will not adversely affect the wages and working conditions of similarly employed U.S. workers. This is typically done through a process of advertising the job opportunity and conducting recruitment effort to find qualified U.S. workers.

If the DOL approves the employer's application, the employer can then sponsor the foreign worker for an employment-based immigrant visa, which would allow the worker to live and work permanently in the United States. The PERM process is often the first step in obtaining permanent residency or a green card for foreign workers.

For startup employers and employees, it's important to note that if the employee leaves the company, this application will not be usable for any other person. If an employer lays off or terminates the employee, the employee must start afresh with another willing employer. If the I-140 is approved, the employee may keep their place in the line or priority date.

General guidance:

For employers, PERM is a costly and time-consuming process. Startup companies can create internal policies on when they would offer to sponsor foreign talented workers for permanent positions. Some large companies do this immediately when the employees join. Some small to medium companies, and startups will have policies that allow them to observe the worker for a year and then take on the burden of the PERM process. Recently, some startups have made the promise of the green card/PERM as part of their invitations to join the company. Whatever you choose to do, let the business needs drive the decision.

Basic overview:

In simple and broad terms, all the preparation, information and documentation needed in the PERM application process can fall under one of three general categories:

1. Employment: In sum, the Department of Labor will want to know the exact duties of the position, the educational and experience requirements for the position, whether there were applicants who were American workers who were "minimally qualified"—meaning that they met the basics of the job description; and that the sponsored employee meets the requirements. All scrutiny is on the job itself. The DOL form is ETA 9089.

2. Employer: Once the DOL certifies the Form ETA 9089, the next step is to file a Form I-140 with USCIS. The most important item USCIS will need are the documents regarding the company financials to determine whether the employer has the ability to pay the salary promised in the PERM. These documents can include tax returns, payroll taxes, bank statements, financial statements, etc. So, this stage is mostly about the employer.

3. Employee: Once the I-140 has been filed by the sponsoring employer, the employee can submit the Form I-485, the green card form. The timing of the filing will be dependent on the country of birth of the employee. If they were born in India or China, there may be many years before the employee can do this. But nevertheless, when that time arrives, USCIS will focus on the eligibility of the employee. Did they violate any visa rules in the past? Have they committed crimes? Only if the USCIS is satisfied that the employee is eligible for a green card, will they be approved for one.

Who should apply for a PERM?

Employers who want to hire foreign workers for permanent positions in the United States should apply for a PERM. The

PERM process is a requirement for employers who want to sponsor foreign workers for an employment-based immigrant visa, which is also known as a green card.

The PERM process applies to most employment-based green card categories, such as EB-2 and EB-3, which require a job offer from a U.S. employer. Before applying for a PERM, the employer must first determine if there are any qualified U.S. workers available for the job. This is typically done through a process of advertising the job opportunity, conducting recruitment efforts, and failing to find a U.S. applicant who can fulfill all the duties required by the job.

If a company is unable to find any qualified U.S. workers for the job, it can then submit a PERM application to the U.S. Department of Labor (DOL) using Form ETA 9089. The DOL will review the application and determine whether the employer has met all of the requirements for sponsoring a foreign worker for permanent residency.

Foreign workers cannot apply for a PERM on their own. They must have a job offer from a U.S. employer who is willing to sponsor them for permanent residency. Once the PERM is approved, the foreign worker can then apply for an employment-based immigrant visa, which would allow them to live and work permanently in the United States.

What are the challenges with the PERM process?

This is a very complex process, and I do not recommend you try this on your own. An immigration lawyer can help a company ensure it follows all the right steps and documentation for the PERM process, and can also help a company navigate any challenges that might get the application denied—a setback for the company and the employee.

Challenges can arise from either the process or with the employer's business situation—or both. For example, during recruitment, if a qualified American worker applies for the position, the employer must either stop the PERM process, or hire both the American and the sponsored employee, in order to continue with the PERM process. Another complication can arise from layoffs, similar to what we have seen during the 2022-2023 financial downturn. The employer may pause the process in compliance with DOL regulations meant to minimize job losses for U.S. workers.[1]

The PERM process can be complex and time-consuming, with several challenges that employers and foreign workers may face:

1. Recruitment requirements: Employers must conduct specific recruitment effort to demonstrate that no qualified U.S. workers are available for the job. This can be a lengthy and costly process, and employers must also carefully document their recruitment effort.

2. Wage requirements: Employers must offer foreign workers a prevailing wage that is equal to, or greater than, the wage offered to similarly employed U.S. workers. This can be challenging for employers, as they must determine the appropriate wage level for the job and ensure compliance with wage regulations.

3. Legal requirements: The PERM process is subject to a variety of legal requirements and regulations, including the rules surrounding job postings, recruitment, and documentation. Employers must ensure that they are complying with all of these requirements to avoid potential delays or denials.

4. Processing times: The PERM process can take several months or even years to complete, depending on various factors such as the complexity of the case and the workload of the government agency processing the application. This can be challenging for employers and foreign workers who are waiting for the approval of their applications.

5. Denials and appeals: Even if an employer and foreign worker have completed the PERM process correctly, there is still a chance that the application may be denied. In this case, the employer may need to file an appeal, which can be a complex and time-consuming process.

Overall, though challenging, quite often the PERM is the only way for startups to permanently hire who they feel are the best employees for their positions, regardless of a worker's country of origin. Definitely review the EB-1 and National Interest Waivers as additional options. And if you proceed with sponsorship, it is important to carefully navigate the process to ensure success.

ADVOCACY AND CONCLUSION

23

IMMIGRATION REFORM

The advocate and activist in me cannot write a book without discussing the need for immigration reform. Every voice is important and so is yours. It is especially important for businesses to speak up. Otherwise known as "corporate advocacy."

The Startup Visa:

The current legal framework of the U.S. immigration system was created in 1990. But as you know, the world order has changed many times over. And, our laws have not kept up with the modern needs of businesses, such as having a startup visa or even these days, the trending "nomad" visa.

I invite you to read my first book in this series *The Startup Visa: Key to Job Growth & Economic Prosperity in America* to understand all the issues surrounding why we need a specific visa for startup founders.

At the end of this book, I've also included some of my previously published articles from *Above the Law*, a legal news and analysis website where I have a regular column. The pieces cover this topic, laying out how and why startups and entrepreneurs should take an interest in comprehensive immigration reform. Many thanks to *Above the Law* for permission to reprint them here.

You will find these articles likely resonate with you and will give you ideas to find your own unique voice.

A merit-based immigration system:

Immigration reform as a whole needs our voices. There are many reforms that need to be made so the process can address modern needs. The process for filing green cards is expensive, tedious and very lengthy—whether it's for yourself or your employee, and whether you're from India, China, the Philippines or anywhere else. The current process of Permanent Labor Certifications should be reformed to having a merit-based system. A change like that would save time and costs for all employers, but startups specifically would benefit.

The visa number of 140,000 is not enough, especially with the decades-long backlogs in the United States. The 2013 immigration reform bill that passed in the Senate, indeed addressed "merit-based" immigration. It would have created a new point-based system similar to the ones in Canada and Australia. However, it did not make it through the House.

The system we have now, which requires employers to prove the position cannot be filled, is unnecessarily difficult. It needs to be changed. Below is a link[1] to my blog post on June 10, 2013, with a summary chart of the bill's provisions. It's time we changed the system to something that works for the 21st century.

Country Quota and visa numbers:

The U.S. immigration system has 140,000 employed-based immigrant visas or green cards a year. Each country in the world is allowed up to 7 percent of the quota. And, that number is further divided by the various categories - EB-1 to EB-5.

In the early 2000s, due to bureaucratic inefficiencies, some of the visa numbers had not been used. Those visas are generally referred to as "unused visas." It is estimated that about 200,000 or so, visas were unused. In the 2020 Covid-19 Pandemic, there were likely more visas unused also. Distributing these visas back in the pool will make a difference to the lives of people waiting in the so-called "line." We must advocate for this, but your voice is more important than ever.

H-1B visas:

I've not talked too much about H-1B visa reform in the past. However, the time has come to discuss it. The H-1B visa is for skilled immigrants coming to the U.S. to perform a job that requires a minimum of a bachelor's degree. Prior to the Trump administration, we lawyers would have to spend months preparing for H-1B applications that would be filed on April 1st. We would have to submit a fully prepared application with the full filing fees totally $1,710 to $2,460. And add $2,500 if you wanted a fast response. It is a once-a-year application process.

The visa starts from October 1st. And any work visa can be filed six months in advance—which is April. However, the Trump administration made a drastic change and essentially required only the submission of the name of the sponsoring employer (petitioner) and the employee (beneficiary) for $10.

This opened the floodgates and suddenly there was a spike in the application numbers because it seemed more affordable. But as a result, the number of applications received increased exponentially and in 2023 over 780,000 were filed. As such, small businesses and startups missed out from the application.

Going forward it will be challenging to "win" this lottery. And something has to be done by Congress.

But keep this in mind—when congress changes anything in immigration law, it comes at a price. So, we do need to be vigilant in our advocacy.

General immigration reform:

No matter how your life touches immigration, all of it needs updating. I have clients who have successfully obtained DACA—or Deferred Action for Childhood Arrival. In essence, those who arrived in the U.S. as children of undocumented immigrants, are effectively allowed to live and work in the U.S. if they meet certain requirements. There are many DACA recipients who would be worthy of a startup visa. Read my article titled "*DACA Entrepreneurs Must Have a Path to Citizenship,*" which is an example of why we need immigration reform from this perspective.

Those aren't the only areas in immigration law that need an update. Another example is asylum law. It is a controversial subject matter plaguing every administration. But in 2022, the Biden administration proposed a rule in which every business—including startups, would be required to pay $600 for every work visa or green card application it files.[2] In other words, Congress' failure was going to be carried on the backs of the businesses of America relying on foreign talent. Though the USCIS requires more funds, businesses should not be the one shouldering that financial burden. Congress must find ways to support immigrants who have been displaced by war or political persecution, without using U.S. businesses and entrepreneurs as a vehicle to raise the money to pay for it. While the proposal has not become law, it is still being considered and has not gone away. Therefore, it is crucial you be vigilant and advocate for yourself where possible. This proposal makes the asylum law problem a business immigration problem too.

Action items:

Here are a few things you can do to advocate for the changes you want to see.

- Sign up to our *Watson Immigration Law Blog* and to my column in *Above the Law.*
- Observe how your cases are going and note the frustration points. Share those inefficiencies with colleagues and your community—basically talk about the problems. Your first hand knowledge is important to share.
- Talk to your congressional representative.
- Write letters to the editor with your local newspapers.
- Talk to reporters and the media. Share the stories and problems.
- Collaborate with, and support others with, the same goals such as trade associations or advocacy groups.

Comprehensive immigration reform will help us solve many of the problems in every aspect of the immigration system as it stands and we must all come together—not be in silos anymore.

24

CONCLUSION

The U.S. immigration journey is challenging for anyone, but particularly so for international startup founders and entrepreneurs. In the absence of a startup visa, we have to navigate the options that currently exist.

I hope you will be able to use the strategies and tips in this book to create your own personal plan to fulfill your dream—whether it is to have a successful startup, or it is to live and work in the U.S. (or both).

If you find this book useful, please share it with your friends, your family, your employers and colleagues, your accelerators and incubators, with your universities, leaders of regional economic development programs, any law and policy makers, and just about anyone in the startup ecosystem you know. It's a starting point and information everyone needs.

Thank you.

ACKNOWLEDGMENTS

For me, a working mother, wife, law firm owner with a busy practice and case deadlines, bar association president, committee member of various organizations, columnist for *Above the Law*, and more that I am likely forgetting at the moment, writing a book like this requires a lot of help: help finding the time and space to write, help with completing action items under any of the hats I wear, and lots of love and encouragement. For each of these responsibilities, I have what I call "villages." And without my villages, I would not be able to serve my purpose in life.

Thank you to my incredible husband, Tom Watson. Tom is one of the managing partners of a boutique patent law firm, Amin, Turocy and Watson, LLP, headquartered in Cleveland, Ohio. He works very long hours remotely from Seattle at this stressful job. But somehow he is still able to be a loving, compassionate and generous partner who plays the juggling game with me equally, if not more. Our girls are at the age where they need shuttling around from activity to activity and Tom shares in all of these life's actions with love and joy. He's built me a podcast studio and a writing room in our house so I can keep serving people as effectively and efficiently as possible, and every time I tell him I have to leave town to speak at a conference, he sends me off with his blessings and says, "Be your best self and come home safely." Ruth Bader Ginsburg had Marty, Amal Clooney has George and I, Tahmina, have Tom.

Thank you to my beautiful daughters Sofia (13) and Sarina (10) who inspire me to be the best mother and role model I could be. They are my muses. I love that they know that my writing time is essential and they accommodate me, and often take charge of their own needs. I am so grateful to them.

Thanks also to my mother, siblings, parents-in-law, and grandmother-in-law, for the unconditional love and encouragement.

My law firm team is my second family. Without their love and help—especially when I have ambitious fantasy-like ideas that I need to fit around a busy schedule—I don't know if I could have written this book. They made sure that I could find dedicated time to write, while also ensuring all our clients receive the best quality work a law firm can deliver. A special thank you goes out to Nicole Lockett, Chief of Staff and Office Manager at Watson Immigration Law; to Cyril Payuho-Sanchez, our paralegal; and our legal assistants Sañata Li-an Dawa and Lance Abadies. Thank you to my former assistants, Cambria Judd-Babbitt, who is currently crushing law school, Alyssa Ortiz who, inspired by her experience at our firm, decided to go to law school and is now practicing law. And to Taylor Phillips who after being a legal assistant with us, went to law school and is about to be admitted to the Bar.

While several friends and clients have asked me to write this book over the years, the first person to emphatically suggest I write this book, is my dear friend Nicole Hay. Around 2013, Nicole, a corporate lawyer, was the first person to read the manuscript of my first book *The Startup Visa: Key to Job Growth & Economic Prosperity in America,* a book that makes the (still relevant) argument that the U.S. needs to reform its immigration laws in order to meet the needs of modern entrepreneurs seeking the American dream. Nicole was so loving, kind and gentle in her explanations of why I also should write a visa guide book for businesses, workers and corporate lawyers navigating the immigration process. At the time, she was working with a lot of startups as their corporate lawyer and could see the need for this book first hand. But I had a one-track vision and mission—I wanted to help change the law and create a new visa category—the Startup Visa. Sometimes I feel defeated in those efforts, but I know I've made a difference with my advocacy. So, better late than never. Ten years later, Nicole's words turned from whispers in my ear to a loud, loving call to action. Finally, the seed she had sown all those years ago, has turned into this book. In the interim period, Nicole, a beautiful soul herself, is now a published author with several other books in the works. You can find her book *Lightwork: Poetry for the Sensitive* on Amazon.

I thank all my clients for giving me the honor and privilege of working with them over the years. This entire book is written through the experiences of being on their business and immigration journeys right alongside them.

Every person who has come across my practice, startup or not, has been a blessing and a teacher, and their energy is within the pages of this book.

My village of startup friends, client-turned-friends, advisors, collaborators, mentors and cheerleaders for this book and inspiration include: Brent Butler, Michele Carney, Becky Carlson, William Dean, Brad Feld, Gavin Johnson, Sridhar Katta, Chelsea Linder, Craig Montuori, Venkat Narayan, Neal Mody, Veronica Palicos, Joel Paget, Cruz Peinado, Doug Rand, Natasa Radulavic, Heather Redman, Surya Rao, Michael Schutzler, John Sechrest, Steve Tobocman, Shahzad Qadri, Troy Vosseller, and Katrina Zafiro.

Thank you to those who read this book in advance and gave me feedback. Special thanks to Craig Montuori, Steve Tobocman, Aijan Isakova from Global EIR and Global Detroit, and thanks to

Maria Pasos-Núñez, Career Advisor, Stanford Graduate School of Business.

Thank you to my editors at *Above the Law,* Staci Zarestky and Alex Dering, and to *Above the Law* for the privilege of being a columnist and permission to reprint some of my articles in this book.

Writing so many columns, OpEds and books simultaneously, needs a village by itself. I love and miss Lornet Turnbull so much, my confidant, writing mentor and very dear friend. I wrote more about her in the dedication near the front of this book. Lornet's spirit is with me and cheering me on, I am sure. Someday, I might figure out how she can be my "ghost" writer. But in her absence and with Lornet's blessings, Venice Buhain is my new editor for whom I am so grateful. She seamlessly stepped into Lornet's big shoes. Venice, currently a journalist with Crosscut, was the editor for The Seattle Globalist, an impactful publication in Seattle for which I used to be a columnist. Venice also helped with my book *Legal Heroes in the Trump Era.* I am grateful the universe brought her into my life.

Caroline Doughty was my godsend when I was writing *Legal Heroes* in 2020 during the middle of the global pandemic. Since then, she's become a friend and trusted advisor, helping to plan and to publish my books. This is the third book we are working on and she brings a whole team of talented people including Libby Hawken, Mim Harrison, Raffy Ferras Hoylar, and Keith Doughty. Caroline's trust and belief in my potential to bring change in this world increases my confidence every time. I am grateful she is part of my village.

Finally, a huge shout out to my friends both in real life (IRL) and on social media who cheer me on in my bird and wildlife photography. [1] My photograph fills my soul and refreshes my energy to pour love into all my other work, including this book. Some of the people who are part of my birding village include

Jigna Patel, Joan Tierney, Ravi Sanga, Jubilee Seth, Christine and Peter Carr, Judge Deborah Fleck, Alisa Brodkowitz, Amanda Dubois, Erin Marie Meyer, Marco Scanu, and Woody Wheeler. Woody is the author of the wonderful book *Look Up!: Birds and Other Natural Wonders Just Outside Your Window.*

And thank you to all of you reading this book. I hope you will share this widely.

RESOURCES

ENDNOTES

WHY THIS BOOK, WHY NOW?

1. http://www.paulgraham.com/foundervisa.html
2. Listen to Brad Feld in his own voice about why the startup visa advocacy is important to him: https://www.startupvisa.lawyer/1906908/9795477-brad-feld-foundry-group-partner-techstars-co-founder

2. PREPARATION GUIDANCE

1. On March 16, 2023, USCIS released new guidance on "ability to pay" https://www.uscis.gov/policy-manual/volume-6-part-e-chapter-4
2. https://abovethelaw.com/2023/01/uscis-proposed-fee-increase-with-new-additional-asylum-costs-will-hurt-businesses/

7. F-1 AND OPT STUDENT VISAS

1. https://studyinthestates.dhs.gov/sevis-help-hub/student-records/fm-student-employment/f-1-optional-practical-training-opt
2. https://www.ice.gov/sites/default/"les/documents/Document/2016/
3. mavniFactsheetDSO1.pdf
4. https://www.e-verify.gov/
5. My Book

8. THE INTERNATIONAL ENTREPRENEUR RULE

1. https://abovethelaw.com/2021/05/biden-revives-the-internationalentrepreneur-rule/
2. https://www.uscis.gov/policy-manual/volume-3-part-g-chapter-2
3. https://www.uscis.gov/i-864p
4. https://watsonimmigrationlaw.com/2013/06/05/invest-visaentrepreneur-visachart-startup-visa-eb6-x-visa/

9. H-1B VISA & CAP-EXEMPT H-1B VISAS

1. In the United States, the fiscal year starts on October 1st
2. The 8 C.F.R. §214.2 (h)(4)(iii)(D)(5) The rule states that 'for purposes of determining equivalency to a baccalaureate degree in the specialty, three years of specialized training and/or work experience must be demonstrated for each year of college-level training the alien lacks.'

10. GLOBAL ENTREPRENEUR IN RESIDENCE PROGRAM

1. https://www.globaleir.org/board-and-advisors/
2. https://www.inc.com/zoya-hasan/-is-the-administrations-entrepreneur-rule-shortchanging-the-american-dream.html
3. https://globaldetroitmi.org/
4. https://thelandcle.org/stories/welcome-to-cleveland-a-new-path-for-international-entrepreneurs-to-build-businesses-here/

12. E-2 TREATY INVESTOR VISA

1. https://travel.state.gov/content/travel/en/us-visas/visa-information-resources/fees/treaty.html
2. https://abovethelaw.com/2022/02/small-alabama-towns-overzealous-traffic-cops-also-monitored-internet-traffic-to-threaten-critics-of-the-corrupt-pd/

13. O-1 EXTRAORDINARY ABILITY VISA

1. https://www.uscis.gov/policy-manual/volume-2-part-m-chapter-4
2. https://www.whitehouse.gov/briefing-room/statements-releases/2022/01/21/fact-sheet-biden-harris-administration-actions-to-attract-stem-talent-and-strengthen-our-economy-and-competitiveness/

15. IMMIGRANT VISA BASICS

1. https://travel.state.gov/content/travel/en/legal/visa-law0/visa-bulletin.html
2. https://abovethelaw.com/2022/02/the-immigration-journey-of-an-entrepreneur/

16. EB-1A EXTRAORDINARY ABILITY

1. **Kazarian v. USCIS, 596 F.3d 1115 (9th Cir. 2010)** ("Kazarian")

19. EB-2 NATIONAL INTEREST WAIVER

1. *Matter of New York State Dep't of Transp* ("NYSDOT"), 22 I&N Dec. 215 (Acting Assoc. Comm'r 1998).
2. *Matter of DHANASAR,* 26 I&N Dec. 884 (AAO 2016)

20. EB-2, EB-3, AND EB-4 PREFERENCE CATEGORIES

1. Amerasians in this context are defined by the USCIS as adults who were born in Korea, Vietnam, Laos, Kampuchea, or Thailand after December 30, 1950 and before October 22, 1982, and who were fathered by U.S. citizens..

22. PERMANENT LABOR CERTIFICATIONS

1. https://observer.com/2023/01/google-pause-green-card-filing-layoff/

23. IMMIGRATION REFORM

1. https://watsonimmigrationlaw.com/2013/06/10/immigration-reform-merit-based-points-system-flowchart/
2. https://abovethelaw.com/2023/01/uscis-proposed-fee-increase-with-new-additional-asylum-costs-will-hurt-businesses/

ACKNOWLEDGMENTS

1. https://tahmina-watson.pixels.com/

ORIGINALLY PUBLISHED IN "ABOVE THE LAW "

A Startup Visa: Now or Never?

When I started my firm in 2009, I had no idea that 12 years later I'd have two books behind me and would be obsessed with changing law and policies.

As an immigrant, an immigration lawyer and an entrepreneur, I get to see up close the incredible contributions my clients make to this country every day. They're creating jobs. They're innovating. They are making a difference.

During the 2008 recession, when many employers were laying people off, I had many clients and had met many international entrepreneurs who wanted to start their businesses in this country —but couldn't. They couldn't because a suitable visa for startup founders didn't exist. And it still doesn't.

Something similar, but on a lesser scale, occurred at the onset of the Covid-19 pandemic last year. All of this has led me to become a fierce advocate for the Startup Visa.

In 2009, a bill was introduced in the U.S. Congress to address the issue and at the time, the idea for such a visa was still new. It wasn't long, however, before the value of such a visa became obvious and the idea took hold, spreading widely, beyond the U.S. By opening doors to international entrepreneurs, countries began to see immigration as a tool to boost their economies and create jobs.

Canada copied our first standalone startup bill, which Congress had introduced but failed to pass in 2010, and used it as a template to create its own. In 2013, that country implemented a startup visa which has generated economic and job growth. Since 2013, Canada has netted $3.7 million in capital investment and 68 new startups.

Many countries have since come to recognize immigration as an economic growth strategy. By 2015, when I wrote my first book, *The Startup Visa: Key to Job Growth & Economic Prosperity in America,* there was a growing number of countries with Startup Visas or some variation of them. Chile is a great example.

Startup Chile's VisaTech Program offered $40,000 of government funds to entrepreneurs who would build their companies there and hire local residents. As the program developed, not only did the country's economy benefit, a new generation of Chileans also benefited by learning from foreign talent. Many of the recipients of the grants are now homegrown entrepreneurs who have learned about entrepreneurship and innovation. The results transcend the economy. The program has been replicated across the world from Brazil to South Korea and more.

In 2021, we have renewed hope for congressional reforms, and it is essential the startup visa be included. However, the immigration reform bill introduced in Congress in February 2021, excluded any such a measure. And even though President Biden revived the Obama era International Entrepreneur Rule, it is a regulatory stopgap. Without becoming part of the law, the regulation can be changed by future administrations.

As we try to ease our way out of this recession, we need jobs for Americans. While there needs to be a multi-strategy approach to job creation, immigration must be one of the strategies. And within that framework, the Startup Visa is a crucial element.

For these compelling and urgent reasons, **the second edition of my book, *The Startup Visa,*** is out today. **There's an** accompanying podcast series **with leading national figures** who all confirm, from their various perspectives, why we need a startup visa.

Coincidentally, the Immigration and Citizenship subcommittee of the House Judiciary Committee of Congress, held a hearing on July 13, 2021, titled Oh, Canada! How Outdated U.S. Immigration Policies Push Top Talent to Other Countries. Led by Rep. Zoe Lofgren of California, who in the past has introduced several measures to address this gaping hole in the immigration system, the hearing was informative and eye-opening.

Witnesses included Stuart Anderson, Executive Director of the National Foundation for American Policy, Jennifer Young, CEO, Technology Councils of North America, and **Dr. Sudip Parikh,** CEO and Executive Publisher, Science Journals, American Association for the Advancement of Science.

Their written testimonies and the recording of the hearing can be found here. I am proud that an advanced copy of my book made it into the record for this hearing.

Ms. Young stated that, "[t]he United States is experiencing boiled frog syndrome. In 2019, foreign-born entrepreneurs in the United States declined by 4,400, the first annual drop since the year 2000. We have been allowing other countries to pick up speed slowly but steadily, to the point where more than 25 countries have modified their immigration policies to attract highly-skilled immigrants and startups."

Mr. Anderson gave examples of founders, such as Zoom founder Eric S. Yuan, who had to "overcome the archaic system we have rather than use the immigration system in a positive way that a Startup Visa could do." He noted a study by NFAP and the Kauffman Foundation that predicted Rep. Lofgren's startup visa bill would have created between 1 million and 3.2 million jobs for Americans.

It is important to note that some House representatives stated that Americans see immigration as one big issue, most of it about the border. In my opinion, if people aren't equating immigration with the economy, it means that more education is necessary to demonstrate the direct and unmistakable correlation.

If you are an immigrant, or somebody who cares about immigration; if you are an entrepreneur, a co-founder, or someone with immigrant heritage—whether first generation, fifth or 10th generation—I invite you to listen to the podcast episode by Brad Feld which was released today in honor of the book launch.

Co-founder of Techstars, Venture capitalist, author of multiple books on startups, and managing partner at Foundry Group, he wrote the foreword to my book. He talks about his own immigrant heritage, the talented entrepreneurs that inspired him to think about the Startup Visa and all his efforts to date. You will be inspired by his storytelling ability.

I hope you will read the book and agree that there's no question that it is time for a Startup Visa -- in America, for America.

Through Tears and Laughter, Celebrating America with my Clients

As an immigration lawyer, I take my clients through some of the most important journeys of their lives - their visa, green card, and citizenship applications. Being in America, to make their American dreams come true starts with their successful immigration applications. And when those applications are successful, I feel all their joy, relief, and aspirations.

On Independence Day, which comes on the heels of the National Day of Joy last week, I want to take a little time to share some of the special moments of joy and excitement from my clients.

The very first time I had to drop the phone because the screeching on the other end was piercing my ears, was when my client "Mary" had just heard the news that her green card application was approved. Mary was a battered wife of an American citizen. She had suffered severe physical and emotional abuse by her husband, who left her abandoned, with no way to provide for herself. He didn't complete her immigration process.

It is not uncommon to see that abusive spouses will often use immigration as a power tool. In any event, she was a lost soul dealing with difficult challenges by the time she and I met. It took a couple of years during which she barely made it through each day. When I called her to give her the good news, I just remember a deafening scream - a scream of joy. It took a good minute before I stopped hearing the loud scream from the handset laying on the floor. I knew that her life from that moment would be changed forever.

Mary's story taught me that experiencing a client's moment of pure joy learning a green card/visa application had been approved, is a true privilege. So, at our office, we take turns to share good news so that I don't hog all of those fabulous moments to myself.

When "Ana," a Roma minority from Bulgaria who grew up persecuted, won her asylum application, she almost made Nicole, our Office Manager and Senior Paralegal, deaf, too. She was overwhelmed with relief and joy. Nicole later shared how emotional she felt knowing she was able to help bring safety and security to Ana's life. All that Ana wanted to do was live her life freely and America gave her the opportunity where she could be herself without restrictions.

Talking of freely being yourself - my client "Tony," who was born in Russia, was able to successfully prove his life would be in danger in Russia because gay people face serious persecution there. When we gave him the good news, I didn't hear a deafening scream. Instead, I heard the deep sobs of a grown man who finally felt he was free to live his life.

My client, "Andy," who founded a start-up a few years ago, had raised a substantial amount of funds. He and his American co-founder had created a pathway to make a difference in the lives of college students in the U.S. His visa application was denied twice before the universe connected us. After a lot of challenging work, his visa application was approved. This very bright, smart, intelligent, and soft-spoken man was not openly demonstrative. When my assistant called him to give him the good news, he was happy to hear it but because of his stoic personality, we were unable to *hear* his joy. But his excitement came through loud and clear in a gratitude email he later sent. He can now take his company to success. Because in America, entrepreneurs can make their dreams come true.

One of my fondest and most insightful memories is when my client "Jenny's" citizenship application was approved. The case fell into a legal exception that we don't get to see often. Even the immigration officer felt compelled to brainstorm the issue at the interview, it was that interesting and challenging. The hard-fought case got me an invitation to her naturalization ceremony. I had never been to one at that point. I saw the entire family go back and forth from happy tears to loud laughter. It was such a privilege to experience that with them. This client's family was in the healthcare industry making a profound difference every day in the lives of Americans and people in other parts of the world.

But it wasn't until my own naturalization ceremony that I came to appreciate what Jenny felt the day she took the oath to become an American. What all my clients feel in that moment. To me, processing my own case actually felt like processing someone else's file, as I went through each required step. In fact, it felt so routine I even told my husband not to bother taking the time out of his busy day to attend my naturalization ceremony. He didn't listen to me and attended anyway. And I was sure glad he did. I sobbed through the whole ceremony realizing all the dreams that I had growing up were being realized in America. It felt like a rebirth. And every 4th of July, I cannot help but think of that day. You can read the detailed story here.

Over the years, I have had the true privilege of hearing screeches, screams, laughter, happy sobbing, happy crying, laughter while crying, and ugly crying when I have had the privilege of telling my clients their immigration case had been approved. Those moments are in fact, indescribable.

It is because America is still the land of dreams. In this country, we can all be our unique selves, while still collectively being American. I love the children's book 'We Are Americans' written and illustrated by Nikita Vyas Hattangady. In her book, she illustrates people from 37 different countries, with different names, languages, and more to demonstrate the beautiful melting pot that we are.

And even though our country faces some serious challenges, at least for now, the American dream is still alive. I take this moment to celebrate my husband who was born on July 4th and overrode my objection to ensure he was by my side during my own naturalization ceremony; I celebrate each and every one of my clients who gave me the privilege of sharing in their immigration journeys and special moments; and I celebrate America for giving the hopes and dreams of freedom and liberty to people, not just in America, but around the world.

ORIGINALLY PUBLISHED IN "ABOVE THE LAW"

Recapturing of Unused Visas is an Economic Necessity For America

I spoke with my clients Jason and Mike the other day. Both have similar issues and they are exemplary of thousands of immigrants in the same boat

Jason and Mike both came to the United States from India as students over fifteen years ago. They completed their STEM degrees and went to into the tech field working at large tech companies in Seattle. They both successfully transitioned into the H-1B visa which is for skilled-professionals. Their respective companies applied for green card applications—which is a long drawn out process of proving the companies couldn't find American workers for those specific positions. The applications were approved, which then allowed both Jason and Mike to extend their H-1B visas beyond the six years allowed on it. That's where the problem really starts.

Those born in India, China, Mexico, and Philippines have to wait significantly longer for an employment-based green card than citizens of other countries. This is because the U.S. immigration law allowance has a quota of 7% immigration from each country in each year, which is distributed among an annual number of 140,000 visas. That number is also divided into categories; EB-1 to EB-5. For example, if you are a Noble Prize winner or *extraordinary* person, then there's generally no waiting time, other than how long it takes to process the case regardless of which country you were both in. If you have a Master's degree or five year's experience, then you are in the EB-2 or second preference category, which has a waiting time generally of 10+ years if you are born in India or China. The wait is even longer for the third preference category. Therefore, there are thousands of people like Mike and Jason in the waiting line.

Law says that all of these visa numbers must be issued annually and any that have not been used, must be rolled into the next year. In the early 2000's, due to administrative reasons, there were about 300,000 that were not used. And in 2012, those numbers became very clear. At the time, there were some discussions on how to get these numbers back in the pool and I wrote significantly about them arguing that the administration should recapture through an executive order.

But in the meantime, the systems were better and green numbers were to be utilized. Until Covid-19 hit. All the embassies around the world and immigration offices in the country, were closed. And therefore, green cards in all categories could not be issued. As such, there were large numbers that went unused.

This fiscal year, there is the fear of the same thing happening. The United States Citizenship and Immigration Services wants to issue all the numbers by September 31st 2022, before the end of this fiscal year.

However, for Mike and Jason, the issue is not as simple. In 2021, because of the above unused visa issue, the EB-2 category was longer than the EB-3 category. USCIS advised that people in the EB-2 category should *downgrade* to EB-3 and flocks of people did that immediately. The result was that the EB-3 category instantly got clogged. And the waiting continued.

In the meantime, the EB-2 is now current, but Mike and Josh cannot easily go back to EB-2 (where they had originally started) because they had some job changes occur requiring procedural notification to the USCIS. That job change then causes a delay in the procedures and which will not allow Mike or Jason to utilize the window of opportunity that is presented.

Mike and Jason are two brilliant minds. Moving jobs within the company or to go another company, are options they have had to grapple with for a decade. Dream jobs have come and gone, but they have not been able to make their dreams come true.

There is a direct family impact too. Until recently their spouses didn't have work authorization, but President Obama did create new rules that provided that opportunity. However, as Covid-19 backlogs began to pile up, their spouses' work authorizations were taking over a year to be approved.

Additionally, Mike has a child who is about to turn 21 and will not be able to be included in the green card application when he turns 21. So, Mike has additional stress about what to do. Mike has contemplated leaving the United States for Canada, like many others who have already done so.

People like Mike and Jason are assets to the American workforce. And keeping them here is beneficial to all Americans. When it comes to their employers; the employers spent significant funds, on average about $15,000 to apply for the green card, then to keep renewing the H-1Bs and then not being able to promote their loyal and experienced team members because all their immigration work could be in jeopardy. This is not good for the businesses at all and thus also not good for the economy.

Some in Congress do recognize this. However, when it comes to immigration bills in Congress, either in the House or the Senate, they don't seem to go far in completion. Currently the Eagle Act seeks to recapture visas and most recently, an Appropriation bill sought to that too. But, it's hard to say if they will pass at all.

In the meantime, Mike and Jason and thousands of people like them including their employers, face despair and frustration.

What can we do? Without Congress passing a bill that allows a recapture of all unused visas and a reform of quota allocation, or a simple removal of the quotas, there will not be a real solution. It is likely that you know someone affected—whether an employee stuck or a business that employs them. So, the only thing you can do is support their voices and advocate for change.

How Harnessing International Talent Can Help Drive Economic Growth

For years I have been advocating that immigration can be a powerful tool for economic growth. Now I have the perfect example to share.

In Detroit, Michigan, there's an organization called Global Detroit, an economic development initiative that centers immigrant inclusion as an economic growth strategy. Located in a city that in 2013 became the largest in the U.S. To file for bankruptcy and led by Steve Tobocman, a former Michigan state representative, Global Detroit operates programs that focus on global talent, immigrant entrepreneurship, and neighborhood development, while exploring how research, communications, and policy can be utilized to build vibrancy and inclusiveness into the regional economy.

In 2019, it launched a Global Entrepreneurs in Residence (Global EIR) program to assist immigrant startup entrepreneurs in the Detroit area.

The original Global EIR Coalition had been created about a half-decade earlier by startup immigration policy strategist Craig Montuori, Techstars co-founder Brad Feld, author and renowned venture investor at Foundry Group, and Harvard Business School lecturer, author, and Flybridge partner Jeff Bussgang. The Global EIR model utilizes a category of uncapped H-1B employment visas reserved for universities, to allow entrepreneurs to divide their time between working at partnering universities and raising funds to establish and grow their own startup firms.

The first university to turn the model into reality was the University of Massachusetts – Boston's Venture Development Center. Initially led by William Brah, and now by Bala Sundaram, vice provost for Research & Strategic Initiatives, the VDC has supported 81 founders who have raised $1.5 billion in venture capital and created some 2,500 jobs. Sundaram told me that the program is so successful that they cannot keep up with the applications from both entrepreneurs and investors who want to participate.

Aijan Isakova, the VDC Program Director, is now working with Global Detroit as the Global EIR National Peer Network Coordinator as the program expands. Already Global Detroit has connected local entrepreneurs with part-time employment at the University of Michigan, Wayne State University, and the College for Creative Studies. In three years, it has supported eight founders from seven different companies who have raised over $15 million and created over 50 jobs.

Additionally, Global Detroit's Global Talent Retention Initiative (GTRI) program has helped Michigan employers hire international students to fill critical talent gaps in the economy. Global Detroit has uncovered a unique set of research data, tracking international students working full-time on the optional practical training (OPT) portion of their student visas, discovering that between 2004-16, over 40,000 international students joined the Michigan workforce in this manner.

That catapulted the state of Michigan into a 10th place ranking among all other states, based on the number of international students working under student visas during the 12-year period studied. The number of international students hired annually by Michigan companies grew during that time by a whopping 330 percent.

In a press release, both the Michigan Lt. Governor and Global Detroit's executive director, expressed their excitement for the immense growth. "Attracting and retaining the talented students at our world-class universities is key to growing our economy, creating jobs, and building on Michigan's heritage of innovation," said **Lt. Governor Garlin Gilchrist II**. "Global Detroit's report highlighting international students' $825+ million in annual contribution to Michigan's economy, shows the importance of building on our budget investment in statewide global talent Retention efforts."

Steve Tobocman, Global Detroit's Executive Director stated: "The State of Michigan's recent appropriation of funds, combined with the region's recent $52 million federal Economic Development Administration grant to build a global epicenter of mobility, will enable Global Detroit, regional chambers of commerce and economic development organizations across the state, industry groups and companies to build talent pipelines that clearly position our state as a global leader in talent attraction and retention."

There are many lessons to learn from Global Detroit. Here are two:

First, though some universities have partnered with Global EIR, more must do so in order for us to realize the true potential and benefit this program can have across the country, to enable talented immigrant startup founders an immigration path for early-stage startups.

Secondly, if states are going to benefit from these programs through the jobs they create, the state must make the necessary investments. They must create and fund programs like Global Detroit. The state of Ohio is doing something similar with its Global Cleveland initiative in the city of Cleveland.

And as a result of the resounding success Global Detroit has enjoyed, Michigan will be investing $5 million in expanding both Global EIR and GTRI statewide, through funds appropriated for global attraction and retention programs in the Fiscal Year 2023 budget passed by the Republican Legislature and signed into law in July 2022.

Detroit's declaration of bankruptcy followed the last recession when the economy was hit hard and needed to find creative ways to revive itself. Realizing immigration as an economic strategy, and creating and investing in programs, was critical for its regrowth.

Now, as we enter another possibly worse recession, Global Detroit and the state of Michigan, are the perfect models to demonstrate how harnessing immigrant talent can bring economic growth to American cities everywhere.

The E-2 Visa and its Potential to Boost the U.S. Economy

If one could have a favorite visa category, the E-2 Treaty Investor visa would be mine. It allows immigrants to establish their dream businesses in the U.S., while also contributing to the economy. Indeed, it is a win-win for all. Unfortunately, the Covid-19 pandemic exposed challenges in this program. But I believe that with some tweaks, the E-2 visa category could be even more impactful, especially at a time when America needs an economic boost.

What is the E-2 Treaty Investor visa? In simple terms, it is an investment *work* visa available to people from a treaty country. A treaty country is one with which the U.S. has a commerce or navigation agreement treaty. Investors and entrepreneurs from these countries can then enter the U.S to develop and direct the operations of a business in which they have invested a substantial amount of capital, usually at least $100,000.

The E-2 visa can be used in any business and in any industry. My clients have been in the tech industry, hospitality, manufacturing, education, supply-chain, apparel, real estate, etc. From startups to big businesses, the E-2 visa can be used across the board.

Generally, the business must have already been established and ready to operate before the investor applies for the visa. In other words, the investment must have been made before the visa application can be filed.

As it has in so many areas of our lives, COVID generated a host of problems for the program. Many embassies and consulates were completely shut down for months, creating a tremendous case backlog. When they eventually reopened, they struggled to catch up and time slots for interviews were extremely limited.

Many investors suffered financial losses because they couldn't physically be in the U.S. In addition, Covid-19 shutdowns across the country affected the profitability of many of their operations. The double whammy dealt a huge blow to many investors, including many of my clients.

These days, depending on the consulate office, interviews can take six to twelve months, resulting in continued financial harm to investors. Yet, these businesses could generate jobs and the tax dollars, the U.S. economy desperately needs right now. Therefore, it is in the interest of America to bring systemic, and policy improvements.

I believe consulates should streamline interviews with E-2 candidates and reduce application packets, which are usually 500-1000 pages long. They could also make better use of technology, by collaborating and tapping E-2 expert officers to conduct remote interviews, thereby reducing backlogs at posts with longer waiting times. Novel problems must have novel solutions.

The treaty country list should also be expanded. With approximately 200 countries in the world, only 80 or so are on the list. The last country to be added was Israel in 2019, but it was a process that took years. Most notably, India and China are missing, yet, both are seeing exponential economic growth. Brazil and Indonesia are also missing. Interestingly, third-country citizenship in order to qualify for an E-2 visa is a growing trend. Some of our clients from India and China for example, received citizenship in Grenada before we successfully obtained E-2 visas for them.

Finally, I believe E-2 visa holders should have a path to legal permanent residency - something that doesn't exist now in any straightforward way. Many E-2 visa holders have been in the U.S. for decades. If they have children who were born here, those children, once they turn 21, would be able to petition for their parents. But those children not born in the U.S. face the 'documented dreamer' problem; they must either return to a country they do not know or change their visa status to a student or work visa. Both are difficult choices and a loss to the visa holder their family, and America.

At a time when the U.S. is facing unprecedented economic challenges and Congress cannot hold any reasonable dialogue around immigration reform, we must look to existing programs, like the E-2 visa, to make them better serve our needs.

Biden Revives the International Entrepreneur Rule

Who loves the Shark Tank? I do! I have watched every episode. And I have learned so much from the show—from what an investor is looking for in an entrepreneur, to delivering the final product to the consumer. I've learned how difficult it is to go from idea to prototype, to raising funds, to solving packaging and manufacturing problems, to getting skews onto shelves and ultimately to success.

I love how human ingenuity can solve real-life problems, generate revenue, and create jobs. As a U.S. immigration attorney, an immigrant, and a business owner with employees, I understand many of the pain points that come with running a business. I get particularly excited when I see entrepreneurs with immigrant backgrounds making their pitches. I'm not only like them in so many ways, but they could be any one of my clients doing the same thing, while also struggling to get a visa so they could do it here in the U.S.

We don't yet have a visa that specifically allows them to do that (read my book, The Startup Visa), but we have a good alternative option sitting dormant and that it appears the Biden administration will revive. The International Entrepreneur Rule (IER) was created during the Obama era, to provide foreign business-minded folks an opportunity to enter the U.S. and put their business skills to work here. The rule is based on existing law and was finalized in January 2017. It was set to go into affect in the summer of 2017 until the Trump administration began the process to dismantle it. Like forgotten bounty, it is now gathering dust, as the mechanism to eliminate it completely was never finalized. As such, it can and apparently is, now being revived by the Biden-Harris administration. What a boon that will be for the economy.

Much like the Shark Tank experience, the IER relies heavily on the credentials and expertise of investors. Applicants will have to show that they have raised at least $250,000 in capital funds from U.S. investors with a proven track record of success. That success will be demonstrated by the investor proving they have invested at least $600,000 in the last five years, and that at least two of their investment companies have generated at least half a million dollars in revenue, or created at least five full-time jobs. Similar to when Shark Tank sharks (the investors) say, "We are investing in you" – the administration wants to feel it can rely on the expertise of the IER investors to know a good business opportunity when they see it.

As an alternative to private investment, the entrepreneur can rely on awards and grants from federal, state, or local government for at least $100,000 for the application.

The entrepreneur must also have at least 10% ownership of the business, and earn a salary while in the U.S. Up to three co-founders may apply for a single startup and the IER visa will allow them each visas with two 2.5 years intervals to stay and grow their businesses. After that, the hope is that the entrepreneurs will change status to a different temporary or permanent visa category.

Why is this important now?

COVID-19 has shown us the important role immigrants play keeping the U.S. functioning during unprecedented and challenging times. It's always been that way. In addition to providing critical, life-giving care throughout the health care industry, immigrants have also been key in other areas, too. Zoom, for example, founded by a Chinese immigrant, has kept us functioning as a country—from schools, to office, to socializing and more. And Moderna, co-founded by immigrants, is literally saving lives through the COVID vaccines it produces.

A 2020 report by the National Foundation for American Policy, found that a startup visa could have created 1 million to 3.2 million U.S. jobs in a decade. And a 2017 report from the Center for American Entrepreneurship found that almost half of all fortune 500 companies were founded by either immigrants or their children. Elon Musk, Henry Ford, Walt Disney, Estée Lauder, Nordstrom, Bose, Levi's jeans, are only a few of the household names that belong to immigrants, or children of immigrants.

While there is new momentum now around immigration reform, the Biden-backed immigration measure, U.S. Citizenship Act 2021, includes no provision for startup founders. And since it appears that with a divided Congress, piecemeal bills will be the way forward, then we will need one for the startup visa, too.

We can get moving on that now that President Biden is taking action on IER, to bring in new, job-creating immigrant entrepreneurs to help lift us out of this depressed economy.

USCIS-Proposed Fees Increases With New Additional Asylum Costs Will Hurt Businesses

The Department of Homeland Security rang in 2023 with some shocking new proposed fees — and a plan to help pay for the humanitarian asylum program with new fees for worker visa applications. On January 3, DHS published almost 500 pages of proposed rules in the federal register, including a list of rising fees, and the big news of a new $600 asylum fee tacked onto employment-related applications. This will be a huge shift and will undoubtedly hurt businesses filing for temporary and permanent visas.

U.S. Citizenship and Immigration Services—the agency that administers immigration benefits on behalf of DHS—relies on filing fees to cover its operating costs. USCIS is underfunded and has called for significant fee increases across almost all immigration forms, including family-based applications.

Some of the fees that apply to businesses and employment-based immigration matters include.

- The H-1B annual registration or lottery fee will rise to $215 from $10. Last year the government received almost 500,000 applications.
- The I-129 form, which is used for any temporary work visa, will have variations of fee increases depending on the type of application. H-1B fees will increase to $780 from $460; L-1 visas to $1,385 from $460; O-visas to $1,055 from $460; and H-2A and H-2B will increase to $1,090 and $1,080, respectively.
- Form I-140, used for employment-based green card (permanent residency) applications, will have a small increase to $715 from $700.

On top of the fee increases, the biggest change is that every application using Form I-129, and I-140 will require the $600 asylum fee, which will go toward adjudicating the humanitarian cases of those who reach the U.S. seeking protection from persecution.

Here's how those fees could add up for one potential employee. With these fee increases, for example, an employer entering the H-1B registration for one potential employee must pay $215 to enter the lottery. If the case is selected, the employer will then proceed to pay a $780 application fee, as well as a required fraud prevention fee of $500, and the American Competitiveness and Workforce Improvement Act fee of $750 to $1,500, depending on how big the company is. The company also will have to pay the $600 asylum fee. And if the applicant needs a speedy answer, there's an optional fee of $2,500 for premium processing, which will be 15 business days for a response instead of 15 calendar days under the proposed rules.

All this doesn't take into account the attorney fees, which can vary from $5,000 to $9,000 depending on the law firm. As such, each employee will cost over $10,000 in just immigration fees.

These will add up very quickly, especially if the business wants to sponsor more than one employee.

These fee increases will have an adverse effect on businesses — not to mention it "robs Peter to pay Paul." USCIS justified the proposed rules with the argument that businesses can absorb the rising costs — even for the unrelated asylum program:

DHS proposes this cost shifting approach with the Asylum Program Fee to place greater emphasis on the ability-to-pay principle for determining user fees. Petitioners for immigrant and nonimmigrant workers generally are required to have the resources necessary to pay the worker(s) for whom the petition is filed, and the fees that the employer must pay USCIS to file a petition are not significant compared to even a small petitioner's revenue and profit.

Nonprofits, small businesses, and farms also face the same new fees for foreign workers, but the USCIS argues that the monetary impact to an individual employer and applicant is small compared with the need to accelerate the processing of the thousands of asylum seekers who have arrived at U.S. borders.

But the reality is that we are going through a recession. Businesses are cutting expenses, and layoff news has been making headlines for months. Just as 2023 began, Amazon announced it would cut 18,000 positions; Microsoft announced 10,000 positions cut; and Google announced a layoff of 12,000. These cuts do not include job losses in 2022. While the technology industry is facing mass layoffs, other industries are seeing an impact, too, including the financial industry, such as Goldman Sachs, which has been planning thousands of layoffs nationwide.

Experts say more job losses are on the way, and thousands of skilled immigrant workers have been laid off as well.

My clients are generally start-ups and small to medium businesses. I know these fee hikes will be a financial burden that will affect their bottom lines. Coming out of the pandemic, businesses have already suffered financially and have not yet recovered. A record number of businesses in every industry are suffering from a severe labor shortage. At a time when businesses are struggling With finances, hiring, and stagnating revenues, do they really have the ability to pay for such high fees?

In my opinion, they do not. Instead, businesses — and thereby the economy — will continue to suffer. The ultimate loser is the American consumer and the American economy.

The truth is that USCIS needs the funding desperately. The rules state clearly why the funds are necessary — from backlogs to systemic issues, there are deep problems. In fact, our entire immigration system has been broken for decades, though the general public has become increasingly aware of the growing problems in just the past few years. But the solution is not to charge businesses more and break their backs. This is a problem that Congress must solve.

Yet, because members of Congress are more interested in fighting than fixing the country, USCIS is placing the burden on U.S. businesses and their immigrant workers. The situation is unfair to everyone in the immigration system — including USCIS, businesses, and any individuals trying to get through it.

The problem is too complex to have any simple solutions. We must have comprehensive immigration reform. But in the interim, USCIS should consider having a tiered fee for the I-129 based on the size of the business. If there must be an asylum fee, make it $200 and not $600. Also, USCIS needs to be held accountable for the fees it collects. And lastly, businesses should speak up against these fees and advocate for immigration reform. If there was ever a moment when businesses need to step up their advocacy, now is the time.

DACA Entrepreneurs Must Have A Path To Citizenship

A path to citizenship for undocumented people in the U.S. has been debated for decades. The urgency has never been more clear than it is right now. Unfortunately, however, with midterm elections around the corner, any meaningful discussion on immigration reform will likely fall onto the "talk later" list. But lives and the economy can no longer wait for "later." Entrepreneurs who are Deferred Action for Childhood Arrivals (DACA) recipients, specifically, are a category of people who can help boost the U.S. economy. Here's an example of one of my clients capable of doing just that.

Andrew came to the U.S. as a child in the early 2000's and started his own trucking company around 2005. In 2012, he successfully obtained DACA status.

He operates in a relatively rural, agricultural area and transports products across the country. He also helps local farmers distribute their crops and produce to major retailers. Andrew's company employs about 20 full-time workers and several contractors. At present, the company is valued at almost $2 million.

He is well respected within the business community. His clients include companies with instantly recognizable names. He is a competent and accomplished entrepreneur.

Andrew is also involved in community and volunteer work. A church-going man of faith, he lives with his wife and three minor children. He embodies all the recognizable marks of a good citizen.

Before the COVID-19 pandemic, the type of work Andrew does was something we largely took for granted. Products showed up on the grocery store shelves when, and in, the quantities we needed them, and we thought little about the process that made that possible.

But the pandemic exposed the importance of every link in the supply chain. From cars and car parts, to baby formula and computer goods, the supply of consumer products across the board are feeling the pinch.

While there are many domestic and international reasons for shortages of everything, the trucking industry remains a key and vital part of the system. And it is facing an uphill battle.

In November 2021, the New York Times reported that the U.S. is short 80,000 truckers, a number set to double in 2030. Think about our supply chain problem doubling as well, and you will begin to see why people like Andrew are such an important part of the solution.

Like most DACA recipients, Andrew wanted to find a way to make his status more secure and permanent, and I explored every visa option and every waiver that might be available to someone in his position.

Working with many startup companies, I pride myself in finding the best visa option for my clients, particularly for entrepreneurs. I often wake up in the middle of the night with a bright-light moment for how to solve some complex visa puzzle.

But in the end, the law is what it is, and my hands are often tied, preventing me from being able to help the people I want so badly to see succeed. Without immigration reform that includes a path to citizenship, there is no legal trick or magic wand that can help people like Andrew become a legal permanent resident or a U.S citizen.

A New American Economy report shows that there are more than 1.2 million DACA-eligible residents in the United States. They had a total household income of almost $24 billion.

In 2015, a total of 37,813 of them — people like Andrew — owned their own businesses, with a combined income of $658.7 million. No doubt that number had risen significantly in the seven years since the report was published.

John Feinblatt, president of New American Economy, said, "Dreamers are job creators. They strengthen businesses and start their own at a high rate — further proof that keeping Dreamers here and hard at work makes economic sense for America."

It certainly does.

At a time when our immigration system is completely broken, and the economy continues to struggle, we must look to legal and policy infrastructures to get us back on track. Immigration reform in general and a path to citizenship specifically, are necessary so that entrepreneurs like Andrew can remain in this country, continue to grow their businesses and create jobs and thrive — to the benefit of our economy.

Time To Step Up Your Advocacy On Immigration

The U.S. Senate last week unveiled a budget framework that establishes "lawful permanent status for qualified immigrants." After years of stagnation, it presents a moment of hope for millions of undocumented immigrants working without legal status in the fields and in the service industry, and in construction, and elsewhere across this country. Only time will tell whether it will lead to real change. But as members of Congress work out the details, there are things you and I can do to help build and drive momentum. Here are three:

Call your representative. No matter the issue, the people we elect to office should be our first line of contact on matters that are important to us and our communities. They want to know what their constituents, (that's us), feel about a topic. So, call their offices—locally or in Washington D.C.—and share your thoughts. As lawyers, our voices can help make the difference when our clients are afraid to share their stories publicly for fear of reprisal. Or maybe you're not an immigration lawyer, but a family member or friend of an undocumented immigrant or perhaps you're helping in other ways, through advocacy or direct assistance. Show your support; be that voice. Call or email your Congressional representative and share your point of view. Here's a link to find and connect with your representative.

Ask your clients to share their stories. There is much fear within the immigrant community, especially among those who are undocumented. Understandably, there is fear in publicly sharing stories. But without those stories, the average person who doesn't think about immigration on a regular basis cannot fully appreciate why immigration reform is important. Help immigrants understand how to better, and more safely and effectively, share their experiences. Maybe you are helping a business owned by an undocumented immigrant who has created jobs for Americans. Have them describe how that helps the local economy. Or maybe your client is from a mixed-status family, with a U.S. citizen spouse or U.S. citizen children. Help people understand how their leaving the U.S. would tear that family apart.

Share your opinions in your local publications. Letters to the editors can be impactful and, indeed, an effective advocacy tool for busy lawyers. Most local newspapers will welcome your thoughts in 200-word letters. This type of advocacy can be quite efficient as it allows you to share your thoughts and opinions on a complicated matter across the broad segment of the population. You are used to writing lengthy briefs and memos anyway, so such letters will not be particularly onerous on your time. If even a fraction of us did it, I have no doubt it would be impactful for raising voices, showing support, and even educating people through different perspectives.

While President Joe Biden has kept his promise to introduce a bill for comprehensive immigration reform, the future of that bill is less than certain. However, Congress is obligated to address the nation's budget, and now it appears using that process to help solve our chronic immigration problem, is possible.

How And Why We Should Recapture Unused Visas To Reduce The Green Card Backlog

The comprehensive immigration reform bill introduced recently in Congress, addresses some important issues that have long demanded attention. One such issue is recapturing unused visas.

"Unused visas" generally refer to the visa numbers that, primarily in the late 1990s and early 2000s, ***were never issued*** for any number of reasons, including because of bureaucratic, administrative, and systematic errors. There are over 200,000 of them, likely more, and they can be recaptured to reduce the current backlog of immigration cases waiting to be processed.

Section 3101 of the U.S. Citizenship Act 2021 bill seeks to recapture visa numbers "lost to bureaucratic delay between fiscal years 1992 through 2020." This is important and necessary.

However, the future of this reform bill, which President Joe Biden fully backs, seems uncertain, at best, given the lack of bipartisan support. Lawmakers have carved out piecemeal bills from the broader measure that are now being considered by Congress. One is to legalize DREAMers, has long enjoyed wide support both inside and outside Washington. Another is for farmworkers, whose role in helping to feed Americans has become even more critical during the COVID-19 pandemic. If piecemeal bills are ultimately how immigration reform will be achieved in Congress, then we'll need a separate bill to address the visa numbers.

In fact, a Senate bipartisan bill was introduced in March 2021, seeking to recapture 40,000 unused visas to be distributed to nurses and doctors. The visas are needed to address what the Department of Labor has declared a shortage of medical professionals during this pandemic. Titled "Healthcare Workers

Resilience Act," the bill seeks to recapture 15,000 visas for foreign-born doctors and 25,000 for nurses. A similar bill was introduced in May 2020, but didn't pass. It is hard to know whether we'll see progress on one this year.

In my opinion, when Congress passed the Immigration Act of 1990 in which these visa numbers were first established, it crafted language to ensure no visa would be left on the table. Rather, it intended that unused visas from one fiscal year would be added to those in the following fiscal year. That makes perfect sense and there is indeed a formula within the law for recovering unused visas. And while I'd love to see Congress reclaim *all* these lost visas through legislation, I believe Biden can also do so through administrative action.

Why is this important now?

When I started my law firm, Watson Immigration Law, in January 2009, it was the height of the 2008 recession. Seattle, where I live, is headquarters to several major global companies, including Microsoft, which hire large numbers of talented high-skilled immigrants, many on temporary work visas, or H-1Bs. For them, the economic downtown was not kind. Many found themselves suddenly laid off and facing the very real prospect of having to return home. Some were in "line" to receive legal permanent residency, or green cards — a laborious process in which employers test the market for qualified U.S. workers before filing the final green card application on the immigrant workers' behalf.

That line, generally referred to as "the backlog," is the time it takes for a green card number to become available. It's often longer than a decade. Sometimes many decades, in fact, depending on an immigrant's country of origin. Yet, if they do not have valid work permission afforded them through the H-1B or other work visas, simply being in line doesn't grant them the legal right to be in the United States. They must always have a valid work visa to be working and living in the United States. A similar scenario played out, to some extent, for H-1B workers, including those in the green card line, as the COVID-19 pandemic triggered an economic downturn in early 2020. Some found themselves laid off by employers struggling financially to stay afloat

What I heard repeatedly from many of these laid-b H-1B workers—more than a decade ago and again more recently—was that they had always wanted to start their own companies, their own startups. Many were talented, skilled workers from India or China, with education and experience in science, technology, engineering, or math (STEM). For them, the green card line can be as long as 20 or more years. They could not start their own companies because a suitable visa did not exist for them. And it still doesn't.

I told every one of the workers I spoke to that I would research to see what could be done for them — if anything. And I've kept that promise.

My research was far-reaching and extensive, taking me down a policy rabbit hole which eventually led me in 2015 to write the book, *The Startup Visa: Key to Job Growth & Economic Prosperity in America*, which was launched at the tech conference, South by Southwest in Austin, Texas. The second edition to that book will be released in summer 2021.

All that research confirmed what my practical experience was already telling me. We have hundreds, if not thousands, of immigrants with an entrepreneurial spirit, biding their time as high-skilled workers, when in fact they can be creating new companies and generating jobs and revenue if U.S. immigration laws would get green cards into their hands more quickly. As a result, I have become a dedicated advocate for recapturing unused visas from past years.

That need became even more evident during the tumultuous four years of the Trump administration. High-skilled immigrant workers came under attack in a very visible and targeted way. Almost overnight, they and other visa holders faced arbitrary visa denials as new policies, particularly the "Buy American, Hire American" executive order, created stringent interpretations of the law and regulations, sometimes downright beyond their authority.

While those policies produced a new wave of immigration litigation, many visa holders were not spared, especially during the first 18 months or so of the Trump administration. H-1B visas holders, in particular, who had been in the green card line for years, even decades, now had to return to their home countries after their cases were denied—forced to leave behind all they had built here. Some owned houses and had U.S. citizen children who had known no other life. Some were able to come back after appealing or filing a new application, but far too many were not. Had they been green card holders, maybe recipients of those thousands of unused visas instead of waiting in that interminably long line, they would have at least been spared some of Trump's wrath.

But the visa backlog not only affects high-skilled workers, it affects all categories of immigrant-visa applications. Family members are often waiting 15, 20, or even more years to receive their green cards. And most wait outside the country. Recently, a friend drew my attention to this tweet which, in part states, "My dad just received a letter saying he could begin the process to try to get my uncle papers. My dad filed the petition 23 years ago. My uncle just passed away." Sadly, this is a common scenario. Even worse is that when the sponsor dies, the application dies with them. This is one example of far too many deep-rooted immigration problems affecting families.

For Biden, recapturing unused visas through executive action, as I believe the law allows, not only solves many of these problems, but frees up Congressional lawmakers to deal with the plethora of equally important issues that can only be addressed through legislation. The time for bold action is now.

ORIGINALLY PUBLISHED IN "ABOVE THE LAW"

The Immigration Journey Of An Entrepreneur

One of my favorite clients recently successfully sold the company she had built from scratch. She inspired me from the moment I met her almost 10 years ago. Most people associate startups with tech companies. But her business was not in the tech field; rather, it was in the now-beleaguered supply chain industry that is bedeviling the world economy.

The immigration journeys of people like Anna (the name I'll use for this article) aren't the ones people get to see or understand. You won't see their stories playing out on the evening news; seldom are they the inspiration for immigration protests and rallies. The U.S. currently has no clear path for entrepreneurs who want to come to the U.S. to grow a business here; rather, there's a mishmash of nonimmigrant visas that allow them a limited presence in the country—if they're lucky.

A startup visa like the one recently introduced by House Speaker Nancy Pelosi, The America Competes Act of 2022, would address this immigration vacuum and many of its symptoms I address here. It would also eliminate much of the uncertainty that arises from both the immigration perspective, as well as the practicalities of operating a business.

I want to shed some light on the life cycle of this journey, with its many twists and turns, using Anna as the manifestation of so many of my entrepreneur clients who have created startups here and are making a difference in this country.

When I first met Anna, she was CEO of a foreign company with many U.S. clients—quite common in today's global market. With such companies, there often comes a point where it's imperative for the owner to be closer to clients, to meet them on short notice when necessary. Anna was at that stage when she reached out to us a decade ago; we sorted through the alphabet soup of visa options available to people in her position. There were two: the E2, or investor visa, renewable every five years, and the L1A, which allows an intracompany transfer to the United States. We opted for the latter, which was more straightforward.

I remember when we first sat down to talk to her about her job duties as part of the application process. Like most successful professionals, she didn't think to list all the things she does in her position as CEO. They were so second nature to her she believed they must be obvious to everyone else. But for the purposes of this particular visa, used for the transfer of executive- and management-level employees, whether someone is performing the duties of an executive is a crucial fail/pass test. I spent a lot of time asking questions such as: "Do you make decisions about the budget?" Her response: "Well, of course, I do, I'm the CEO." Gradually, we were able to demonstrate on paper what she did in real life and her L1A was ultimately granted.

But for new companies in the U.S., an L1A is given for only a year. That meant that pretty quickly, we had to file an application to renew it. She was able to add two more years to her U.S. stay.

In the meantime, her business was growing and she needed more help from people at the mother company who knew the operations inside and out. We were able to successfully obtain another L1A for key personnel.

Anna's expanding business soon began attracting the attention of bigger firms in her industry. One of the things most founders will tell you is that their exit strategies are often precarious because they lack permanent immigrant status in the United States. Even if a new and bigger company buys them out, most founders would have to stay on for at least a year or two to ensure a seamless transition. And with the limited types of visas available to founders, there isn't always a good option for obtaining permanent residency, (a green card) in the United States.

We were lucky, however, because the L1A does have a path to a green card, referred to as an EB1C. So, we began the process of applying for that

As immigration attorneys, we always have to remember that our clients are people with personal lives, not pieces on an immigration chessboard. And personal issues arose for Anna that challenged and tested the process all along the way.

Eventually, the time came to meet with an immigration officer for the final interview. There are many questions she and other founders at this stage are asked to assess their worthiness of legal permanent residency in the United States: Is she indeed an executive of her company? Has she committed any crimes in the past? Finally, the officer approved the application, and we all left the U.S. Citizenship and Immigration Services offices beaming. But our celebration was short-lived. As I got to the parking lot and started my car, the immigration officer phoned me. He told me he wouldn't be able to grant my client a green card because there were currently none available. The government had halted all green card issuances for that day

I was stunned.

As immigration lawyers, we learn about the availability of green cards through what's known as the visa bulletin, issued by the government around the middle of each month to forecast visa availability in the month ahead. But I cannot recall a time when the bulletin was implemented immediately.

We were in a holding pattern because there were no green cards available. Anna had to wait almost a year before she could actually be issued one. In the interim, she could continue to function fully under her L1A status which had to be renewed for another two years. For other founders, the wait for a green card to become available could be anywhere from two to over 20 years, depending on their country of origin and category of green card application.

Throughout all this, discussions about the sale of the company were in full motion. The L1A manager, who had been transferred in to help run U.S. operations, was nearing the end of their tenure, and we needed to find a way to keep them here The immigration laws for successor entities in an L1A to EB1C situation, is not as straightforward as it is in other visa to green card categories. In addition, there are myriad implications with buy-in from future owners, not the least of which is whether they're even willing in the first place to navigate this visa process for an employee. In this case, fortunately, the new owners have assumed all obligations giving us a path forward.

As the immigration lawyer in these cases that involve other attorneys, financial experts and other professionals, my ultimate responsibility is ensuring everyone's immigration status remains intact throughout the life cycle of the company. Ensuring everyone involved is aware of all the visas in play and that they all understand what would need to happen in a transition, merger or acquisition is a crucial part of the process. I essentially take on the role of a juggler: executives at the target company need to be reminded about immigration deadlines and other issues; those acquiring or merging with the company need to be aware of the immigration obligations involved. For Anna's company, the immigration strategy was fully implemented and became part of the understanding of the sale.

It should be noted that a startup visa would consider this successful sale as part of the positive evidence for immigration purposes.

Life is constantly throwing us curve balls. But Anna handles her business and the personal challenges that come with it, with savvy competence and graceful leadership. She has created hundreds of jobs in the United States — both directly and indirectly — and has contributed to the economy in so many ways. She is the example of the American Dream that our founding fathers aspired to, to make America a place for all.

ORIGINALLY PUBLISHED IN "WATSON IMMIGRATION LAW"

Invest Visa Senate Amendments: A Proud Moment for Watson Immigration Law

Today is a very proud day for Watson Immigration Law.

Our readers will know that the Startup Act has been a passion of this law firm for the last several years. So, when the comprehensive immigration reform bill S.744 was released, we wasted no time in diving into the details of the Invest Visa. You may recall our summary, our analysis and our chart. We immediately followed up with the Startup community to get their feedback. We have spent many a night on this very issue. It was through this passion that arose the opportunity to assist Senator Moran's office with their amendments. We are proud to have had the great privilege of working with Senator Moran's office in helping improve the bill. The provisions will undoubtedly help the American economy by creating jobs at a time when it is so necessary. The provisions will help retain brilliant minds (that we might otherwise lose to Canada and their Startup Act! Don't miss the bill board image in the memo!). The provisions will also help immigrant entrepreneurs achieve their American dreams. It is a win-win for everyone, if you ask me!

I want to take this opportunity to thank the Senator's office and his staff, for the tireless efforts on this issue. Jason Wiens, the Legislative Director, deserves a special thank you for his dedication and hard work. Thank you for letting WIL be part of this venture.

I must also thank two important people who have been superstars on this issue for several years. Craig Montuori,the founder of Politihacks and Munly Leong, an entrepreneur himself. They both manage the popular website www.startupvisa.com. Their Facebook page has almost 4,000 very active followers. Our complimentary skills and knowledge helped us accomplish this huge goal. Thank you Craig and Munly, for your incredible insights, knowledge and dedication to this cause.

I also want to thank our clients who have participated and supported this huge task. We really needed your support and you gave it to us!

Yesterday, the amendment was filed! Today a press release was issued. Now comes the time to vote on the matter. Every vote matters. I urge you to call your senators and ask them to vote yes to these amendments! If you are a STEM degree student or graduate, or you are visa holder with ambitions of having your own startup, you must call your Senator!

PODCASTS HOSTED BY

TAHMINA WATSON

YOU CAN FIND THEM ANYWHERE YOU LISTEN TO PODCASTS

INDEX

M

N

O

P

ABOUT THE AUTHOR

Named a Top Immigration Attorney for Startups in America by *Business Insider*, Tahmina Watson is a nationally recognized expert in U.S. immigration law. Her specialization in the visa needs of global entrepreneurs has resulted in hundreds of successful startups and millions of dollars of business investments in the U.S.

She founded Watson Immigration Law in Seattle in 2009, bringing to her practice a unique qualification for representing international entrepreneurs: of Bangladeshi heritage, Watson is a naturalized U.S. citizen who emigrated from her native England, where she first practiced law as a barrister.

Watson is among the immigration attorneys that *The New York Times* has tapped for informed perspective on the state of immigration visas in the U.S. She is a sought-after industry expert, speaker, and media spokesperson who has appeared in numerous major outlets including Bloomberg, Forbes, NPR, and CNN. She is a member of the Forbes Business Council and is a columnist for *Above the Law,* which covers the legal profession for business readers. She has also been a speaker at the annual conferences of SXSW and SelectUSA, a Department of Commerce initiative for U.S. business investments.

Watson is a 2023 recipient of the prestigious Apex Awards of the Washington State Bar Association, recognized for her leadership in giving agency to immigrants by providing access to legal assistance.

She has received honors from the Puget Sound Business Journal and the American Immigration Lawyers Association, for whom she has served as a national spokesperson. She chairs the Response Committee of the Association's Washington chapter. Elected the president of the King County (WA) Bar Association in 2022, Watson is also a former president of the King County Washington Women Lawyers Association.

Watson hosts a dedicated podcast on U.S. immigration law for startups and founders seeking visas. This is her second book devoted to the topic. She is also the author of the bestselling *Legal Heroes in the Era of Trump*

Watson lives with her husband and two daughters in a suburb of Seattle. Perhaps because she helps so many investors and startups see their vision for U.S. businesses take wing, she has become an avid bird photographer.

watsonimmigrationlaw.com.

Made in the USA
Monee, IL
24 November 2024

71103395R00134